HOW THIS BOOK WAS WRITTEN

Letter by letter it unfolds - an extraordinary daily gift that Matteo so freely gives the world. Thought-provoking, inspired, pertinent and filled with jewels to help us grow as human beings, this book invites us on a journey. Matteo approaches life from a unique perspective - that from his world of limited-speech autism, and we're allowed to come!

I have a special job as both his mom and one of his letter board facilitators. I type the letters in the computer as Teo points to them on his letter board; I'm basically my son's secretary. I'll tell you what though, I've never before been so excited to go to a job. To hold this "secretarial position" is the biggest honor I've been given, and it has taken me on the most rewarding journey of my life.

Autism has become more of a household word lately, so many of you understand some of the challenges that may be associated with the condition: lack of language and/or an inability to freely express oneself, challenges identifying social cues, struggles connecting the mind and body, underdevelopment of motor skills and coordination, repetitive behaviors (stimming), hand-flapping, and quite often sounds that randomly escape from one's mouth. Oh, and the whole, "Intellectually, your child is functioning at the level of a _____ year old (you fill in the blank with what you've been told about your child)," is so completely wrong!

There are many, many variations on these and additional challenges, but there are also such amazing gifts that we, as neurotypical people, cannot even comprehend. As Matteo says, they are the "best kept secrets of autism."

Our journey began when Matteo was 20 months old and let's just say that it has been a wild ride ever since! Full of ups and downs, twists and turns, and many zigs and zags as we would discover the next step in our journey together. Then we found letter-boarding (we use the SOMA Rapid Prompting Method, specifically), and we were "home."

Our son's world opened, his intelligence, creativity and knowing burst forth, and we were (and continue to be) amazed! We were graced with one surprise after another: ranging from his knowledge of what's going on around him (even if we didn't think he was paying attention), his understanding of what was being said in conversations and that of current events, his concept of spirituality and understanding of God, energy, love, and the universe in general. Matteo made his love of nature, music and art as well as the profound way he experiences each of them, immediately evident in his writings.

You'll see how spiritual my son is as many pieces of writing include the words universe, energy, love and God. He makes sure to let you know that he is non-denominational (see the "About Me" section of his website at www.matteomusso.com for further details and explanation) and that these writings

are not meant to be a "conversion" to any organized religion. Rather, Teo enjoys that people experience love, beauty and peace in many ways, and says that as long as we're all living with love for others at the forefront of our lives, it doesn't matter what that spirit is called out loud. In fact, when he first began speaking spiritually, he capitalized the L in Love, and only later, did he tell me that Love is God. Teo also makes it clear that Jesus is his best friend. When he was non-verbal, Jesus is who God sent as someone who understood Teo in his silence...an answer to Teo's prayers.

As he began sharing this information, I was so thankful that I was only charged with taking dictation because I didn't understand many of the concepts he was trying to express and share. They were so deep and thought-provoking, they challenged me and other readers to look at everyday experiences and things in this world from a different perspective. Not all writings are included in this book, but by popular demand, we've taken many of the most beautiful and thought-provoking pieces and assembled them here for you to enjoy.

Enjoy your own journey!
Many Blessings to You,
Annette (Mom)

This is a compilation of writings over the span of the past three years when Teo was 12-15 years old. We'd stay up until midnight together as the thoughts would just come pouring out. The most amazing thing to me is that they come out perfect the first time! He never corrects a word or phrase; it's just the way it's supposed to be the first time, according to his message. No editing of words has been done, only a rare comma has been added. I always ask Teo if it is OK before adding it though.

I hope you can find personal meaning in many of these writings and that you enjoy Matteo's invitation to perhaps see both simple and some of the more complex things in life through a new, refreshing lens.

If you are interested in hearing more about our journey and reading more of Matteo's insights about autism, please see his first book, *Handbook of Us: Understanding and Accepting People with Autism*, available at Amazon.com.

Enjoy your own journey!

Many Blessings to You,
Annette (Mom)

Copyright © 2012-2019 Matteo Musso
All rights reserved.
No part of this publication may be reproduced, distributed or transmitted in any form or by any means, without prior written permission.

Matteo Musso/Over The Fence Publishing
P.O. Box 2227
Livermore, California 94551
www.matteomusso.com
matteo@matteomusso.com

Publisher's Note: This is a work of fiction.
All brand names and product names used in this book or trademarks, registered trademarks, are trade names of their respective holders.

No warranty, express or implied, is delivered by the author or publisher with respect to the contents of this book.

Moments of Feeling Known: Life Perspectives from an Autistic Teen / Matteo Musso.
-- 1st ed.

ISBN 978-0-9988636-7-2

Moments of Feeling Known:
Life Perspectives from an Autistic Teen

by
Matteo Musso

Love works Best
- teo

Over The Fence Publishing
Livermore, California

I continue to be awed by Matteo's ability to masterfully weave his insightful thoughts with such wisdom, inspiration, and heartfelt emotion. The profound messages he conveys through his writings stir my very soul and empower me to experience life with so much more understanding, kindness, and gratitude for God's blessings.

~ Jodi Lundell

Thank you, Mom and Dad,
for everything.

DEDICATION

I dedicate this book to each of my wonderful therapist friends. I've had so many over the years that it might take three pages to list all of you, but you know who you are.

I have been blessed from having each and every one of you in my life. My journey has been brighter and I've experienced more presents in the form of care, love and nurturing than any one guy can comprehend.

Autism does have its beautiful gifts and you are each a gift to me. I'll always love you and be grateful for your presence and presents in my life.

Love, Teo

Thank you, new friends who have opened these pages as a symbol of opening yourself to a new idea or two.

Reality is so beautiful, when kindness and acceptance is the foundation on which our village is built.

Love and curiosity blend in a crock pot left to simmer on low. Hours upon hours pass, becoming months, then years. All the while, the flavors blending lusciously, until the surprising entrée is complete.

It was not rushed or cooked too fast, for that makes it tough. Instead it simmered, taking all the time given and all the time needed, to develop into a gourmet meal.

Tender and savory, the perfect flavor of love, sautéed with patience, acceptance, joy, curiosity, respect, wonder and divine inspiration.

A meal for the most gracious and cherished of humankind. Welcome to the table my new friends, dinner is served.

Love,
Teo

CONTENTS

NATURE
Energy of the Setting Sun..................................1
Palm Springs Sunset..2
Inspired in Hawaii...3
Leaves Falling in the Breeze..............................4
Bellowing Waters..4
A Special Mom...5
Camping and Crabbing.....................................6
Watching the Evening Surfers...........................7
Yes, Another World..8
Dream Surfing..10
After Whale Watching in Maui.......................11
Seeing This Waterfall.......................................12
Yellowstone National Park...............................13
Unchanged Energy...14
Waves Beckon...16
Goodnight My Sun...18
View From the Top of the World....................19
My Brave New Friend......................................20
A Time to Chill at Bo Beach............................21
Dancing Colors of the Night...........................22

FOOD
Soul Food..28
Ode to an Egg...30
Hot Tamale...30
Sugar Poem...31
On a Chili Night...31
Dining Adventure, Uncle Yu's.........................32
Dining Adventure, Railhouse..........................34
Dining Adventure, Mama's Fish House..........36

Dining Adventure, Panama Bay..........................39
Dining Adventure, Fat Daddy's.........................40
Dining Adventure, Wente Restaurant...............42
Dining Adventure, Sea House............................44
Dining Adventure, Aviation Rooftop................45
Cake Pop Rock...47

MUSIC
Hearing with your Heart....................................52
CLAP!...54
Soul Bathing..56
My Listening Experience, Bach.........................57
My Listening Experience, Haydn......................58
My Listening Experience, Shubert....................59
My Listening Experience, Mozart.....................60
My Listening Experience, Beethoven................61
My Listening Experience, Ives...........................62
My Listening Experience, Mendelssohn...........63
My Listening Experience, Dvorak.....................64
My Listening Experience, Handel.....................65
My Listening Experience, Liszt.........................66
My Listening Experience, Wagner....................67
Musical Review: Marc Cohn Live.....................68
Little Black Dot..71

SPIRITUALITY, GOD AND THE UNIVERSE
Answering God's Call...75
You Are Alive..76
We Are Always With You..................................77
A Poem for the Ages..78
Dark Days..80
I Wait...81
Him..83
The Truth About Silence....................................85

Monks at Holy Cross Monastery................86
Pebbles..87
I Have No Lack....................................88
Human Classroom................................89
Universe Created..................................90

AUTISM
My First Essay......................................94
The Definition of Me............................95
The Puberty Sonnet..............................96
Brainiac Waits......................................96
I Am Not Silent...................................97
Believe in Me.......................................97
Beginnings of RPM Writings................98
Being Autistic....................................100
Note to Sara.......................................102
I Watched Him..................................103
A Tough Road...................................104
Hot Times in our World....................106
Patience is a Virtue, Dear Parents.......107
Our Euphoric Lens............................108
Anticipation of Joy............................110
Dear God..111
The World Awakens to Autism..........112
The Inside of Me...............................115
Autism Awareness Month..................116

MY PRESENTATIONS
Lincoln Center, NYC........................121
Up and Away Performance................123
Dear Hammer Organization..............125
They Came Today.............................126
Jackson Ave. Elementary Talk............128
K.N.O.W..131

MISCELLANEOUS
- Attraction and Reaction..............................134
- Life Victorious..135
- A Night to Shine.......................................136
- For You..136
- More Love Than Hate – 9/11 Tribute.........138
- Artificial Intelligence – AI.........................139
- A Welcome to Freedom.............................140
- Deepening Renewal..................................142
- Learning to Cut the Motor.........................144
- Memorial Letter to Uncle Robert...............146
- Laughing...148
- Exercise Sonnet..149

HOLIDAYS
- A Halloween Story....................................152
- A Thanksgiving Wish................................154
- Inflammation Anticipation........................156
- Thanksgiving 2018 – The Boy....................158
- Smuin Christmas Ballet.............................160
- Christmas Presence 2016..........................162
- Christmas Message 2017..........................164
- Advent Message 2018...............................166
- New Words to Jingle Bells.........................168
- Christmas Message 2018..........................169
- Oh Christmas Treee..................................170
- Christmas Eve Message 2018....................171
- Popcorn in the Sky...................................172
- Happy "Knew" Year! 2019........................173
- Easter Message 2017................................174
- All For One and One For All......................175
- Easter Message 2016................................177
- I Have a Dream 2019................................178
- I Have a Dream, Too 2018.........................180

My Brave New Friend..................................182
Veteran's Day 2018......................................183
You are Brave..183
Mom's Are Beautiful...................................185

ABOUT THE AUTHOR
Matteo Musso..187

NATURE

ENERGY OF THE SETTING SUN
January 2, 2018

Mankind searches for light, yet often languishes on the disappearance of it, instead. To notice a beautiful sunset is simple due to its brilliant colors. But to be aware of its preceding light is often overlooked. Have eyes that are opened wide and in so doing, have hearts that pour out love and comfort to others. Mix the colors and you have artwork. Children mix the colors easily until taught to keep them separate on the palette. "Be careful not to blend them or you'll have a mess," they're taught.

Colors take the form of attitudes, opinions, beliefs and thoughts, even race and ethnicity. Letting the colors blend creates the most beautiful sunsets of all, there for everyone to enjoy. All you have to do is lift up your head and gaze at its beauty. Don't wait too long though, because it is a feast for your vision only momentarily, if you look through your eyes. Once the darkness of night arrives, that beautiful, colorful image must be reflected through your heart to be seen by others.

Bring the light of each new day to each other, and then raise your head and notice when the colors blend at the end of a day. You are the artist that creates the beauty.

May your palette enjoy life's blendings.

PALM SPRINGS SUNSET
March 16, 2018

Each night, the sun retires from our side of the world and retreats to another place, one where it has been before and where it will be welcomed once again. Leaving us last night, the sun waved at us with its magnificent splendor. Calling for support from its friends, the clouds, its intent was to manufacture such an exit as to leave us no other choice than to take pause from our nightly activity, step outside and just look.

If only for seconds of our life, in that still moment, we stood in awe and admiration of nature's beauty and the power it holds for us in our heart, mind and body. All of that inner peace awaits our willingness to seek it, recognize it make time for it, then let it in.

Last night, the pink met with grey and white, hiding parts of itself behind majestic mountains while presenting us with silhouettes of palm trees and tiny birds.

Nature performed a dance of inner peace for us last night. Thank you Mother Nature, for the front row seats you provided for us. Our spirits were touched and our eyes were delighted. And all of this, admission free.

Discrimination does not exist in nature.
Its beauty is available to all who seek it.
Thank you, Mother Nature, for your gifts to us.

Love, Humanity

INSPIRED IN HAWAII
May 4, 2016

Yesterday really was a relaxing day. Changes in my head made me doubt myself, though. Mom stuck adamantly to energy of hope and trust in God's plan, so I am fine now. Sure helps to have Dad and Mom so grounded in their love and faith in me.

That being said, my hope for today is restored and I am confident in my future. The Grand Canyon of the Pacific (Waimea Canyon) was beautiful yesterday. When I saw the waterfall, my thoughts of awe went directly to Christ and God.

"How should we give thanks for such beauty?"
The boy silently asked his friend.
Love comes pouring down with a force that does not end.
To witness such an outpouring is a gift all by itself.
And to share a gift of love with others changes the world
    as you change yourself.
That waterfall keeps flowing through sunny days and
    storms,
Just as the love of our friend Christ, God's son whom
    we adore.

LEAVES FALLING IN THE BREEZE
November 4, 2016

Form: AAAA BBBB

Why do you fall, little leaf?
Don't give your mother grief.
Eat enough and sleep beneath
   the others kindly beds bequeath.
Little Leaf began his journey
   quite excited, it was his turny.
So off he flew, the breeze was surely
   taking him to find a girly.

BELLOWING WATERS
February 9, 2016

Inspired by our hike to Murray Canyon, Palm Springs, California. As we sat resting at the waterfall, I wrote this.

Bellowed the waterfall to the stream,
Understand that we are one and the same.
Different forms we take but of the same energy made.

Now you flow as gently as a newborn baby sleeps,
Down to the valley to nourish life itself.
Will you have the power to kiss all those in need?
I am here for you in strength and plenty
   if you will only call on me for help.
I am the source of your abundance,
And the way to end the thirst of the world.

A SPECIAL MOM

I sit and breathe deep breaths of freshness provided by that Mom who knows our every need, Mother Nature.

She's constantly aware and calls me to receive inhalations of purity delivered in unique ways. Today the mode of transportation is redwood trees. They have accumulated hundreds of years of pure holistic healing energy. Just think...we have to do nothing to receive this gift, only choose to place ourselves in their paths and let our autonomic nervous system do it's thing. Breathe in and out. Let in thanks for the gift. Notice its energy and let its loving spirit enter and heal. Mother Nature, can we respect you enough to cherish your delivery mechanisms? It's the least we can do as humans.

We will protect you, too. I promise.

CAMPING AND CRABBING
Bodega Bay with my Boy Scout troop
November 12, 2016

Crabbing was so much fun.
What an experience.
I felt the ocean's music under our canoes and
the ocean's breeze pushed us to be our best selves.

We had to work together for safety and success
and we shown as bright as an evening sky
with brilliant stars.

As a life lesson, we learned how to work together
as a team to reach a common goal.

I am so blessed to be learning these lessons
with my friends.

Come on guys, let's learn and play some more!

WATCHING THE EVENING SURFERS
May 7, 2016

We were supposed to go on a cocktail cruise on a catamaran this evening, but the waves were too crazy, so it got cancelled. We returned to our condo and watched the surfing show which was going on right outside our porch! Wow…Amazing!

I was inspired to write this lyric poem.

Big surf beckons those whose souls are called to ride. God, restless to heed their call, He graces them with a rush and inner thrill reminding them that they are alive. For those of us who watch, awe and inner peace melt together in a feeling of wonder.

Crash! Slam! The waves crescendo like the most beautiful symphony, romantic and appealing to even the harshest of critics.

The world applauds and promises to care for these musicians and the entire orchestra, so that generations to come may hear this song and feel it's healing energy.

YES, ANOTHER WORLD

Blue with pops of white, constantly they burst.
Rolling blue peaks go up then down,
Living smoothly, calmly first.
I sit and watch it play so sweet,
It's gentle music, with its beat.
No specific frequencies are heard,
Yet I absorb her every word.
I let her message enter me so I can live life peacefully.
Hunt for sounds that beckon you.
Let them in, see what they do.
Too often now we drown them out
    and man-made substitutions shout.
The radio, iTunes, tv, games
    and constant talking replaces claims
    that nature once had owned outright
    and now she battles to restore our sight.
I sit and listen everywhere I go,
A gift of autism others don't know.
They say we're in "another world"
    during these special times.
I am agreeing with them, for sure,
It's the world of the sublime.

I ask of you to try it on
    and become autistic, too.
'Cuz visiting that sublime world
    is peace for me and you.
The blue is nice but I love the pops
    created by water plus the rocks.
The splash sometimes is high then low,
My soul loves both sizes and what they show.

And the people flocked to nature in silence,
And they heard God's voice.

DREAM SURFING

Written after my first surfing lesson with Zak Howard on Maui.
February, 2017

Can you come and play my friend?
Can I tempt you to live an inner dream?
Step off the shore and come to me.
I will protect your body while thrilling your soul.
Do I frighten you my friend?
My sounds can be mighty and my force can get fierce,
But that is not today, my friend.
Today I am rolling and each time I fold, I give you a gift.
Do you want to open me and truly feel what I am?
God wrapped me this morning for you, my friend.
Energy builds up slowly then surprises your senses
    with the ride of your life.
Can you come and play my friend?
Enter the water.
Trust. Breathe. Wait.
I will come to you

May I say, surfing in the ocean of Hawaii is magical. It was like opening yourself up to God and letting His grace into your soul and heart. Can't acquire it without experiencing it first. To watch surfers caress these majestic waves of nature is inspiring and awesome. To ride a wave yourself, with a confident friend like Zak, is akin to doing that which you never dreamed could happen to you. Dream surfing came true for me today and my heart sings.

AFTER WHALE WATCHING IN MAUI
February, 2017
This is about my experience on a catamaran.

So I sat there, consumed by my chicken wings, perfectly happy and at peace on the boat. Then all the sudden it happened. Whales emerged from the ocean like mountains emerge from the sea. The difference
is one emerged in an instant, and the other over millions of years.

Which is more magnificent?

Let's ponder...

Well mother, well baby,
Thank you for your bravery.
Traveling far, under the sea,
What a gift you came to me.
Mounting, mountain, where is your mom?
I long to climb you, big and strong.
You must be brave to stand alone,
Here I come, you feel like home.
How to compare these two dumbfound
    the naturalist in each of us, I've found.
Both are alive and still evolving,
Man's souls still crave that which they're solving.
Whales played and breathed and slapped and breached,
The sight was what God's always preached.

SEEING THIS WATERFALL
Tahquitz Canyon, Palm Springs, California
The waterfall at the end of the hike was barely trickling.

I am never disappointed.
Why would one choose to hike this canyon, get to the end, stand at the base of one of Mother Nature's creations and say aloud, "Well that was anti-climactic"? A lady just did that here. I feel a bit sorry for her because this is what I saw...

Breathtaking cascades flow from top to bottom according to gravity's rules. Coming down constantly, the wet gift flows. Where is the faucet and who turns the spigot? Only mother nature knows. That is a mystery left for us to ponder as we sit and wonder. Understanding may not be the point of the gift. Perhaps it's to give our spirit a lift. Why will so few ponder at all and make instead a hastened judgment call? There are sounds of the stream that don't make me scream. There's a very faint breeze that won't make me wheeze. The sight of the water falling that to me kept on calling. Shade from the sun let my eyes have fun. So I sat there all nestled, respite given my human vessel.

A Note for Humanity: "When the water is low and there's less of a flow, the beauty may change, but it is still there for the chosen ones who seek it. Seek and find, that's the obligation of being human."

Love, Mother Nature

YELLOWSTONE NATIONAL PARK
June 27, 2018

A drive through beautiful pines served as a preamble to some of the most awe-inspiring exhibits of nature I've ever seen. To say that Mother Nature prepared her exhibit like a pro is a gross understatement!

We all know that the curator of a museum plans and organizes their displays so that all may learn and enjoy them. Mother Nature is the master curator. The majestic pines, so great in number that the human eye cannot count, lined the path, taking us to eruptions of steam, boiling sulfuric lava, jeweled water lined with life and a waterfall that roared like the king of the jungle. Earth tones of tan and terra cotta live in harmony with jeweled tones of sapphire blue, aqua and teal. Some had thin layers of yellow…rare, ironically, to Yellowstone Park. Can you imagine, after seeing all these magnificent pools of color, witnessing two separate rainbows painted in the canyon, assisting the thunderous waterfall? As if it needed help displaying its wonder! Mother Nature obeyed God by painting love in the sky.

The Dynamic Duo strikes again!

UNCHANGED ENERGY

Needing solace, I came to you,
Beginning my new day with you.
A comfort you provide for me,
Free of commands and judgments
Just you and me.

Lost in your beauty, I forged on…

Trails provided ups and downs,
Even rights and lefts,
I like your "rights" much better
   than those behind, I left.

Within your canyon walls I moved,
My body obeying my mind.
How do you do that, Mother Nature?
Due to judgments left behind?

Your trails do not demand my silence
   or a proper whisper,
Nor do you adapt your challenges for me
   or test me with silly gestures.

Your trees and stream share their energy with me
   knowing that I understand.
If all people could just experience you
   we'd all live hand-in-hand.

They'd learn to provide opportunities to all
    even without knowing,
What miracles do or do not exist
    inside despite what showing.

Please don't decide what we can't do,
Just learn from Mother Nature.
We may need help going up the hill
but together we can conquer.

Isn't that true for all of us,
We'll rise to goals that are set?
At work, at school, at home or play,
Belief in yourself's the best bet.

Others may not see so well
    but they may think they do.
It's not their fault, they may be trying
    and believe they're helping you.

Today the Canyon provided me
    a wealth of inspiration,
To everyone who comes to me;
Family, friends and those unknown,
I'll be a gift they'll see.

My heart is filled with appreciation for the beauty in which I sat and hiked today. The inspired thoughts that spoke to me are the extra gifts that came my way.

WAVES BECKON

The waves are playing, just as if they are a loving family on an adventurous vacation.

Some smaller and youthful but wanting to mature. These are the playground for natures young, both wet and human. They provide such playful energy. All may enjoy.

Then the next set of waves emerge, reminding all who see them that they are the mature adults of nature. They beckon those who have learned respect and give it unconditionally to those who have earned it.

Waves of this nature are recreation to some and fear to others, thrilling to some and frightening to others. Reality is, that they are the same waves yet solicit a variety of responses within us.

They'll keep coming, these powerful forces of energy, never ceasing to decide who they will be. They will come to us steadily, over and over, just as the seconds of a clock tick their soothing sounds with never ending reliance.

Can we learn the respect required to eliminate fear? If we choose it, then we have blessings rolling toward us, nonstop and abundantly.

Playful versus powerful, enjoyable versus intimidating, those titles disappear and they are all just beautiful waves bringing peace and harmony to those blessed enough to visit.

GOODNIGHT MY SUN

Sunset changing colors, right before you sleep,
Thank you God for giving us a tiny little peek.
It's secrets are still hidden behind the hazy clouds,
While once again it disappears
   with others shares its light.
Where do you go, why do you leave?
Will you come back tomorrow?
I'll miss you while I sleep tonight
   but see you in the morrow.
Get sleep tonight or do you need it?
   our favorite shining ball.
Without you we cannot survive,
Humanity will you call.

VIEW FROM THE TOP OF THE WORLD
July 24, 2017

I studied Mt. Everest and the climbing conditions, and was inspired to write this poem.

Mountain, Mountain at the top of the world
Take care of the climbers, please.
Invited or not they are called to you,
Their curiosity to appease.

They would not appear at your base camp unless
    your call to them was heard.
Your majesty they yearned for in their hearts,
Like God's unwavering word.

How treacherous every foot step is,
But happy is the snow,
Who gets to live forever there,
Unless its smushed by toes.

But if it is, it understands
    its purpose was to help,
The people need to fill their hearts
    with beauty not with kelp.

How can we fathom the tallest one?
Just like we cannot see,
Everest expands out of our sight
    like God's love for you and me.

MY BRAVE NEW FRIEND
In honor of our troops.
September 24, 2017

Thank you, my friend, you are so brave
Your time, gifts and bravery to us you gave.
You've left the comforts of home behind
For the freedom and safety of all mankind.

Why are you willing to do this for me?
Risk your life and your comfort for even those
   who can't see.
I think I know why, or at least I'll guess…
You think more about others, and about yourself less.

Democracy is important to you
It is also to me,
And to thousands of other people,
Who only dream to be free.

With a big sense of purpose and all the right training,
Off to battle you go.
Just know in your heart, your mind and your soul,
That we're with you, more than you know.

And God sent his angels to protect them and help them feel our love.

Your new friend and professional pray-er,
Teo

A TIME TO CHILL AT BO BEACH
Bolinas, California
July 2, 2017

Give me your tired, your lonely, your distraught,
Give me your curious, your energetic, and your whimsical spirits.
I am rest or invigoration for the soul, depending on what you seek right now.
I am wild at times, yet constant and serene at others.
Some appreciate my moodiness and are willing to look inward and discover that we are not that different, you and I.
But others look at my tumultuous exclamations and wonder how such a beautiful creation can change moods in the blink of an eye.
I must alter my state of existence to feel alive,
For how can we appreciate calm, rolling waves unless we experience crashing, thunderous surf?
Without contrasting times, life's games would prove to be mundane.
I am here to experience life, too.
I am affected by moon and universal energy.
But to tame me is to strive for the impossible.
I would never exist to please all at the same time,
For that is also impossible.
Variances in me are what touch the souls of everyone at different times in life.
May you find fulfillment with me throughout your life, as my purpose changes within you throughout the years.
Bring me your heart, your mind, your soul,
And I will give you peace.

DANCING COLORS OF THE NIGHT

Universes collide and particles separate
   and we cannot see all.
Since science has discovered this,
   we realize we are small.
Just lift your eye gaze to the sky to see
   what you can see,
Then realize for a moment how vast
   this place can be.
Some days we have just one to see and
   even then they say,
"Avert your eyes, don't stare at her! Your sight
   will go away."
Just feel her warm embrace instead and soak
   in vitamin D,
On the days she's covered up just know
   it's temporary.
For celestial beauty that's safe to see
   go out in the dark of night,
And look without the city lights
   at beautiful specks of white.

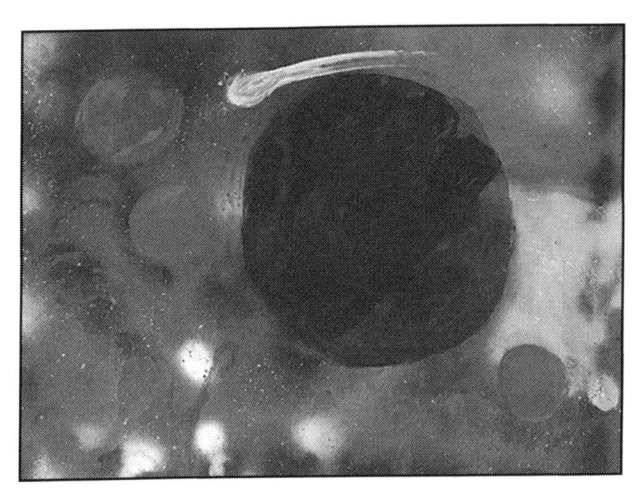

Acrylic by Matteo Musso
"Universes Collide"

Some still choose to understand only what they can see.
If you are one with vision like that, just come hang
   out with me!
The universe has taught us sight is not only one kind.
The depth of any vision has its limits in our mind.
There's much more way beyond, that which lies
   in front of us.
Seeing past the tricks our eyes can play is life and
   love and trust.
And the people took time to look upward
   to the night sky.
Deep breaths of thanks were taken and the night
   showed them red, blue, green, white and yellow.

And the orange danced.

FOOD

Matteo had just given a presentation at
Winona State University. Afterward we were
in the cafeteria and they had an entire table full
of desserts and Teo returned with only
a big plate full of Jell-O.
Here is what he spelled on his letter board as he
was smiling and laughing at his plate:

*"The jello is a ballroom dancing instructor fired
for doing too much hula."*
- Matteo

SOUL FOOD
Published article in *Maui Vision Magazine, May 2018*

Food, glorious food…the thing that sustains life. Many of us have strange relationships with food. Without enough of it, our physical bodies would cease to exist and be unable of sustaining life. Sustenance for our souls is required as well, yet we don't often prioritize it or think of it as essential.

So, check this out: We consistently eat each day; meals, snacks, whatever. If we wait too long, our bodies send us loud reminders to eat. We respectfully acknowledge and oblige. "Num! Here comes some food. Hang in there, Stomach. Help is on the way!" "Whew!" it replies. "I'll stop sending the annoying reminders, then." We are satisfied and our bodies will react in accordance with what we ate. Will we have more energy or feel lethargic? Be alert or groggy?

What we feed our souls also affects us. Spend too much time with people who think negatively and they can drag you down. Those who are joyous can lift you up. So, friends can be a huge meal for us but please notice that you're at a buffet. You get to choose what you put on your plate. Sometimes we keep eating things that aren't healthy for us. Then one day we may notice that we don't feel so good as we're digesting certain foods. Hmmm, do I want to keep eating it?

Well, remember that eating sustains life, but not all food is created equal. When it comes to me, soul food is contained within four major food groups: Spirituality and faith, love of family and friends, the Arts and exercise. Each day, it's important that I fill my plate with a bit of each. The mix can change, but my "soul food pyramid" is always intact. At least, that's the goal.

Music transports me, painting frees me, writing releases me, praying comforts me, meditation relaxes me, exercise grounds me, friends humor me, Dad reasons with me, Mom calms me and love envelops me. Those times when these foods lie synergistically on my plate, I am fulfilled and my soul bathes in a shower of bliss. Then, digesting life's challenges become merely fleeting moments in time, then we return to the buffet for our next helping.

Thank you, Chef!

ODE TO AN EGG

Egg, egg, why are you so hard to eat?
You are soft and slippery, so not hard in that way.
Why then, do I toil when faced with you on my fork?
You are jam-packed with protein and my body craves it,
But my tongue protests and my taste buds cower.
While you may not be my favorite,
I encourage your descent down my esophagus.
I am brave and strong in my teenhood,
 so fear of an egg is gone.
Residue from that childhood tactile fear has lingered,
But dissipates daily.
Can you have patience with me, oh Egg?
I am slowly accepting you and your odd texture.
Mouth is open, insert fork with hitch hiking egg.
It's that simple. Just do it, Teo!

HOT TAMALE
November 4, 2016

Hey, Hot Tamale! Why do you hurt my mouth so?
You started out so innocently as maize and meat,
Then you transformed into something hot, not so sweet.
You want to be eaten, that's proof on my plate,
Can't eat you so fast so at the table I wait.
"Digest now!" I say, to bites inside me.
There's more to come, laugh all you want,
I'll digest you, you'll see!
Well, my plate still has more and you know I can't throw it,
So eat you I will, or maybe I'll stow it.

SUGAR POEM

S Sugar is so sweet.
U Utter the word and I drool.
G Gonna eat some candy,
A And if you give me sugar,
R Really, I will die!

ON A CHILI NIGHT
January 4, 2017

There he stood in the kitchen, Dad in his glory.
He tosses and blends, like a culinary chef's story.
"What shall I add next?" his brain asks with a flurry,
If it's beans, meat and sauce, it becomes chili in a hurry.
Resigned to the pot, the ingredients simmer.
Soon they will become my Wednesday night dinner.

Dad to Mom: How did he know it was Wednesday?
             Who told him?
Me: It logically arrives after Tuesday.

Go down my throat after I chew you
Or I am afraid that I'll have to sue you.
Reluctant it flowed, right to my tummy.
I'm glad that it did, 'cuz it was so nummy!
My hat's off to Dad who created this grub.
Remember this recipe; we'll start a chili club!

Thanks for the loving dinner, Dad.
Love, Teo

Welcome to *Teo's Tasty Adventures*,
where I describe my dining experiences.
I have been lovingly referred to as "*The Poetic Foodie.*"

DINING ADVENTURE #1
UNCLE YU'S, LIVERMORE
June 12, 2018

The Shirley Temple was laced with multiple cherries adding extra flavor for my mouth and a visual treat for my eyes, as the cherries danced in close confinement and proximity to the ice cubes, known as "rocks," in this case.

We had orange peel beef, asparagus beef, beans, lemon chicken, pot stickers and crab and cheese puff pastry.

I think chopsticks are crazy utensils to eat with. Balancing a piece of meat between two sticks requires way too much skill. I'm just hungry…let me get the food deposited in my mouth ASAP! Let's not make it an Olympic event!

The cream puffs delighted my mouth with their crunchy exterior, akin to the house the wolf couldn't blow down in that nursery rhyme. Protected inside was the creamy combo of cream cheese and crab. Hot, delicious residents!

The pot stickers were the best I've had in all my 14 years. Crunchy top, but the rest, smooth as silk. Slippery for chopsticks, so Dad said I could use my fingers. The flavors mixed to perfection and they just slid right down the throat.

Lemon chicken is a favorite of mine. I enjoyed the freshness of the meat. It's tender finish blended with rich and thick lemon sauce. Rich enough but not overdone. A nice choice.

The beans are addicting. Beware of their innocent veggie appearance. Their kicky spice sneaks up on you then grabs your attention. Then "poof," they're gone. You dream of them and crave them the next day. What secrets do they hold?

Asparagus beef is your combination of a blind vegetable seeking stability in the carnivorous world in which it's grown. They dance together in the pan, not as adversaries from two different schools of nutritional thought, but rather as dancers in the Smuin ballet. The costume of sauce, dressing the performers, tastes scrumptious…there in subtlety, not taking center stage.

Want a "desert" meat dish? Want to taste the most original combination of flavors set to a plate? Then order the Orange Peel Beef. It's a rainbow living on your tongue, if only for a few seconds at a time. Eating it will leave a lasting impression on your mouth.

The service was impeccable, the food arrived in perfect time and the atmosphere provided safety for my auditory processing challenges. This restaurant has an energy that said, "We welcome you to Uncle Yu's."
Bon Appetite!

DINING ADVENTURE #2
THE RAILHOUSE
Lake City, Minnesota
October 6, 2018

The Railhouse is the best restaurant I've eaten at south of the Twin Cities, in my professional eating opinion. Let's discuss why.

The chicken quesadilla arrived in a timely manner and on a cool plate, I might add, even though the place was packed. The perfect amount of cheese acted as a casein-laden adhesive holding the beans, onion and chicken together. The other secret ingredients attached themselves like magnets, which assured a multi-sensory culinary experience was available in every bite.

The pretty orange tortillas provided housing for the goodness and at the same time, transportation from fork (or finger), to mouth. Ahhh, the eagle has landed. I did applaud the spinach salad Mom ordered. The chicken lay atop the bed of green, so warm and humble. But its texture and flavor could have commanded arrogance, due to the satisfying and enjoyable effect it had on my mouth and tongue. The added extras of cheese, cranberries and candied nuts (on the side of course, due to my nut allergy) completed the plate of Mom's lunch, which she graciously shared with me.

With love and culinary skill, my stomach was fulfilled once again. If only all the children of the world could have this experience. Just as Chef Doug pours his heart into the culinary delights at the Railhouse, let us all pour our hearts and attention into feeding all people in this world.

There is enough for everyone, why are some hungry?

Happily Yours, with a Blessed Tummy,
Teo

DINING ADVENTURE #3
MAMA'S FISH HOUSE RESTAURANT AND INN
Maui, HI

I love such energy. Mama's family love is felt so much here. There could not be a more gorgeous view anywhere than from right here at our table.

Drink: Lava Flow
The umbrella could not protect the contents of this pretty glass from its destined journey through me. Cold, blended and sweet, it cascaded down my throat all too easily and it was gone in a flash. Don't let me have another, lest my tummy fill up. Heavenly!

A gift from Chef Perry: Mushroom and Clam Bisque
The soup was the texture of silk with the flavor of mushroom delicately sharing center stage with clams, neither of which my palette has experienced much. Why parents, why? Perhaps Chef will give me the Bisque recipe for Christmas!

My favorite was the crab cake. It's outer crunch protected the sleepy white meat which barely required my calcium-laden friends to work. Some taste buds came to life which have laid in nestled slumber far too long. "Num," isn't fancy enough. Perhaps it deserves an ovation!

Shrimp needs no formal introduction. Their filet-cut presentation required them to sit at attention and wait to be appreciated by their entourage of hungry guests. Crunch, followed by smooth softness and dipped in sweet in a sweet pond of sauce. My mouth felt like a prince wearing a crown of jewels.

The crab cake was akin to a favorite cousin, visiting for only a short time, yet our experience together leaving lasting impressions on me.

My entrée gets an encore! The white fish tasted like cumulus clouds waiting to release stored up raindrops of flavor. Bite by bite, the raindrops fell into me, cleansing and delivering the gift of protein to my body. Supported by grains of black rice and veggies, my entrée was the perfect storm!

Dessert, dessert, how do I love thee? More than a summer's rain? I'm afraid so, at least tonight! What could be more delectable than chocolate mousse served in a clam shell cookie house? Resting in a cookie, my dear friend, Chocolate, does not protect you. Did you not learn from your predecessor, Lava Flow, who came to me under an umbrella? I know your true intention was to invite my tongue to sing and my sweet tooth (or "teeth" in my case), to be fulfilled once again.

You are a strong leader, Chocolate Mousse, and your colleagues of Sorbet and Crème Brulee supported your mission with astounding success! If there were a Medal of Honor for desserts, you would receive it!

The food at Mama's needs no kudos from me. It's reputation stands alone and I'm just a kid after all. But I do specialize in reading the hearts of others in this world. From the orange, bouncy energy of the valets, to the first beautiful hostess who took our name, to the warm smiles at the entrance, to Karen, Lisa, Floyd and Chef Perry, it was genuine peace, comfort and happiness from people who love what they do and for whom they do it. And we had yet to even reach our table!

MAMA'S FISH HOUSE RESTAURANT AND INN
Continued...

Our server was awesome and my beautiful new friend was as OCD as I regarding filling my water glass and clearing the plates as they emptied. Since that's my "thing" right now, I appreciated her professionalism more than most. We had the best seat in the house, on top of all the other special treats. And the fresh leis given to us made my heart swell bigger than the Grinch's at Christmas time.

Thank you all at Mama's Fish House for giving me and my parents a royal evening fit for a king. I felt like one of the family. While I may not have arrived on Maui in a boat after years of adventure like your family did, I am blessed to have arrived at Mama's and receive a culinary and emotional adventure of my own.

Mahalo! Love,
Matteo

DINING ADVENTURE #4
PANAMA BAY
Livermore, California

The "Chuck Norris" mango, pineapple smoothie:
I liked it a lot. It fit nicely through the straw and had a direct route to my mouth.

Chocolate Croissant:
The delicate pastry crumbled with elegance onto my lap, but the brunt of it found a quick hiding place in my mouth. My taste buds discovered the flaky guest, then called into action all available chomping soldiers.

Not one, not two, but 20 or more quickly answered the call to action. You must find a way to let my digestive system partake in the job it's meant to do. Chew away my little calcium laden friends, then let the saliva provide transportation to my stomach. "Num," I say. Good teamwork, body.

ADVENTURE #5
FAT DADDY'S, SMOKEHOUSE BBQ
Maui, Hawaii

BBQ, BBQ, how do I love thee?
Well, much deeper after tonight's dinner at
Fat Daddy's in Kihei, Maui.

I'm savoring these wings. What could be better?
The wing's blend of flavors and the way they melt in my mouth like a favorite ice cream, is so special. (Be careful of the bones though if you're thinking about ice cream as you eat these, haha). I must show these wings my respect by cleaning them to the bone!

The beans next; Green and healthy, they cleansed my meat pallet. Crunchy and al dente, they provide vegetarian accompaniment to my carnivorous platter to come.

It sat there, that meat platter, patiently waiting for me. It's succulent inner voice called to mine saying, "I wait, but don't understand how you can!"

Pulled pork ran down my throat, but my tongue snuck enough of a taste to reflect its goodness by watering and anticipating the next bite.

Burnt ends lavished my entire mouth with savory, smoky meat... as tender and satisfying as a warm embrace from one you love.

The smoky finish of the chicken elevated that meat into the "International Taste Olympics," which says so much when sitting beside the next treat; the ribs.

Dad made the mistake in asking if they were better than his. What's a loving kid to say? They're different than Dad's, so I can't choose. Suffice it to say, Fat Daddy's ribs said "Aloha" to my taste buds and they replied with total enjoyment.

Sausage and brisket told their individual stories as they entered me with the justified confidence of prize fighters.

I appreciated the coleslaw between each bite as it cleansed my palette allowing me to enjoy the taste of each variety of meat to come.

Key lime pie and flourless chocolate cake somehow finagled their way into me, even though my tummy was as full as Santa's sleigh on Christmas Eve! Num!! I couldn't refuse their sweet invitation.

You know, the food would be enough to warrant Fat Daddy's a "Gold Star" rating from a typical food critic, but I'd say that what made my dining experience primo, was its welcoming energy and "chill" vibe. Eric and Dan we're so nice, professional and filled with island charm. Chris, the owner, made a special point to come in and speak with me. What a truly genuine heart he has. No wonder I want to return there soon.

Mahalo to all of you at Fat Daddy's!
You sure serve up a smokin' meal!

ADVENTURE #6
THE RESTAURANT AT WENTE VINEYARDS
Livermore, California

Matteo's Drink: Non-alcoholic Garden Mojito with pomegranate, hibiscus, ginger

The mojito was fresh and full of vibrant colors, as the pomegranate mingled amongst the ice cubes with hibiscus and ginger from the garden outside. My throat enjoyed the wet visitor and my thirst was quenched.

The bread sat there waiting. "Will they pretend they don't want me?" the gluten-filled goodness wondered. But I could pretend no longer. Soft and pillowed, the inside lay protected by the crusted army full of seeds and baked to perfection. Crunch – ahhh! Don't forget the olive oil!

The Wente Vineyards Classic Caesar arrived with pomp and circumstance as it's reputation preceded it. No need to be nervous little leaves…you were dressed in a layer of moist flavor and you wore it so well. My taste buds were singing and I must say it was the best Caesar salad I've had in my 15 years of eating.

I loved my Dry-Aged Wagyu Ribeye, as is evidenced by its disappearance. Mom sliced it into bite-sized pieces, so all my energy could be used to savor the flavors. They hid within, danced on top and surrounded the piece of steak which would soon be supplying my body with essential proteins.

But it was much more than that. The texture was like a piece of soft gold, rich and smooth and desired by so many…it's flavors supplied my senses with savory fulfillment.

The Apple Dessert Cake and Flourless Chocolate Cake floated toward my table like graceful angels sent to brighten my day and provide satisfying closure to my evening. Not overly sweet, the desserts said "Good night all, and sweet dreams to you." My taste buds received the encore they craved.

Tonight at The Restaurant at Wente Vineyards, I went on a culinary journey. I went from the glass of cold and wet, through a green leafy jungle, rested upon pillowed bread, walked down a tender meat pathway to the sweet journey's end. I was greeted and waited upon by gentle souls who strived successfully to help us feel welcomed and provided primo service. The chef and pastry chef both came out to greet me and I felt so special.

Thank you all at The Restaurant at Wente Vineyards. Your orchestra of service, talent and the atmosphere of welcoming comfort played beautiful music for me tonight. You blessed my evening…and I am so fortunate.

With a tummy full of thanks,
Matteo Musso

DINING ADVENTURE #7
SEA HOUSE RESTAURANT
Maui, Hawaii

The salad provided a dense combination; so many flavors. It was like a rigorous hula dance in my mouth. I could just order another, but then I'd be too full to enjoy the next culinary surprise. Bring it on, please.

Well, just as I suspected, Chef Alex rocks! He accommodated my nut allergy as I really wanted the basil pesto fish creation. Basil has pinenuts so alas, it was a no go. But I am happy to say that the pine nuts weren't missed. Chef came out and ran his ideas by me, how cool was that? My taste buds are singing the Hallelujah Chorus right now. Thank you George Frederick Handel and thank you Chef Alex.

Here's the thing, I'm 13 years old and Chef made time to come out to my table to make sure I'd have a meal that was safe for me and that I'd love. Wouldn't you say that's a rarity?

The food tonight tasted of skill, talent and pride. The ingredients were fresh, The recipes were creative and the presentation was artistic. But the secret ingredient in my meal that set it apart from all others on my vacation, was that the food was treated like art and loved by the artist.

Chef Alex doesn't cook, he creates. His positive energy is felt in the food and it sure tastes good!

Thanks Chef Alex, the cooking staff and everyone at the Sea House!

DINING ADVENTURE #8
AVIATION ROOFTOP BAR AND KITCHEN
Livermore, California

The H2O was nice and wet, just the way I like it. The lemonade, it evaporated all too quickly due to its slippery numminess.

I enjoyed the Aviator Cheeseburger and the tater tots. They were a nice diversion from traditional french fries. They crunched on the outside; that crunchy layer acting as a noisy down jacket providing insulation for the meat of the tot. I enjoyed a warm tater tot even though I found it necessary to consume my burger in its entirety prior to indulging in the tots.

The Burger:
How do I describe its perfection? The bun; a slight crunch outlined the underside rim as texture number one. Puffy fresh bread surrounded the high-quality meat, cooked to my requested finish. Accompanied by onions, cheese, and other toppings, the flavor and texture combos provided a plethora of sensory experiences for my mouth.

I have thoroughly enjoyed it and will take the extra tots to go please. Thank you for this tasty treat that was my lunch!"

CAKE POP ROCK
August 14, 2017

Cake pops bring a boy such joy
   I cannot hide under my desire.
Let's make our own but share with scouts
   cuz' of sugar, we'll never tire.

Boy finds new energy hidden deep
   within the sneaky pop.
With respect and adoration
   I get to go, not stop.

Hop in my mouth, you succulent treat,
I'll help you if you need it.
A more welcoming mouth you'll never meet,
But it's wanting me to feed it.

No, not with veggies, fruit or meat,
I get enough of them.
It's treats like you who call to me,
My long-lost chocolate friend.

A bad rap you are given without nutrition,
But isn't joy and succulence just a different form
   of nutrition?

I get fed those things from you,
Let the green stuff handle the rest.
It's probably no big secret,
That I like you the best.

MUSIC

MY DEFINITION OF MUSIC

Music is nourishment for our souls with different vibrational speeds and frequencies intersecting to affect us emotionally. Different ones and combinations affect us differently and depends on our own simple caring each day. It also depends on our openness to let it affect us.

Please hear my story, not as a tale of my adventure, but as an experience every human should get to have during their life here on this Earth. Love, Teo

HEARING WITH YOUR HEART

Thump, thump, thump it beats as steadily as a springtime rain. It does so as naturally as we breathe in and out. Reliable, constant heartbeats keep our bodily vessels alive and assure us moments, one after another, here on Earth.

Steadiness is a gift we often forget about day to day, and it takes that unsteadiness to attract our attention and remind us that we are alive and full of living vibrations.

I was recently reminded of this one windy day early in October on the campus of Luther College. So special is this place that my heart was singing all day. As I spoke to two classes of students, I felt their excitement and eagerness to learn about the secret wonders of being autistic. In their backpacks it did not remain but, rather, they wore it on their faces and carried it in their hearts. I felt it and saw the beautiful colors of acceptance and respect for a life led differently than most. Then God brought me a man-angel named Josh as I ate in the Union.

So vibrant was his energy that I would have followed him anywhere, and I did. During the Nordic Choir rehearsal, I followed him right into the bass section and this is what happened next...

Slow, deep vibrations surrounded my body as the basses practiced alone. My heartbeat sped up as each note escaped from those around me. Then the whole choir sang together yet those deep vibrations held me anchored to the core of the Earth. I was safe and secure, more than I have felt in recent months. As I rejoined mom and Anne as an observer, I returned to my chair much more than that. I was now part of them and their beautiful music. I listened to the next song with anticipation of my journey with them, as new frequencies would blend together, bounce off each other, then rest upon each other like sheets of luminous light, created for those blessed enough to hear and experience them.

How blessed I am to have been a recipient of their music, but even more to have been part of it. You see, if we listen with our hearts, our vibrations blend with theirs and love, the highest vibration we can feel as humans, is shared with the world and it becomes a better place for us all.

I wrote this after watching Christian Reif conduct the San Francisco Symphony. I was able to meet him after the concert. He's an amazing conductor and all-around cool guy!

CLAP!
March 3, 2017

One might liken today at the symphony to a novel filled with romance, dancing and peace, lively chatter and erupting emotions. Notice the erupting emotions happened first.

The Barber (Second Essay for Orchestra) was depicting our soul's decision to live, I mean, really live! Should it remain in a state of stagnancy, or should it take a chance on living life to it's fullest?

Our soul holds an inner debate, being introduced to the vigorous ups and downs of being human. Contentment versus challenge, kind harmonies versus dissonance, sweet softness versus loud shocks of jagged sounds, they culminate in a smorgasbord of senses leaving our soul craving more sensations. The rest is over. It's time to truly experience our humanness.

Enter Mozart (Symphony No. 41, *Jupiter*), the first welcome to our hearts. "Welcome. So glad you're here," sing the concierge-like notes of the Jupiter Symphony. Reliable, comforting sounds stream toward our souls with an embrace of anticipation that drives us onward. To where shall I go? The predictable progressions comfort us in this new adventure, giving us energy while providing just enough curiosity and filling our need for growth.

The notes provide safe respite as we know always, that a fulfilling resolution is on the way. Uplifted and confident, we venture onward and dare to seek the most powerful emotion of all, the one that's got the ultimate strength to transform every heart and the entire world, love.

Cheer on Dvorak (Symphony No. 8) for his depiction of love through our auditory system! Storing up note after note in an invisible vat built by God to hold infinite pounds of weightless love, Dvorak seems to get this idea. Keep adding beautiful notes of kindness and chords of good deeds, and the love multiplies. Singing melodies emit tempting lures and we are hooked! We can't help but join in the game of goodness. The sounds are just too beautiful to leave behind, so we follow the guidance of this beautiful music until our hearts are filled with immense joy and a desire to share this feeling with others on our journey. It culminates in us. Then the final exclamation is revealed.

We put our hands together, over and over, making them musical instruments of their own, in an effort to let the emotion out. We want to feel our body again after our emotional emersion, "CLAP." We want to show our thanks and gratitude to composers, musicians and conductors, "CLAP." We want to live life anew and refreshed, "CLAP." But most of all, my hands want to be percussive with thanks to God for my human experiences, especially those today, "CLAP, CLAP, CLAP!"

-Matteo Musso, age 13, pre-verbal autistic

SOUL BATHING
A thank you note I wrote to the *San Francisco Symphony*

Thankful notes released from the pages of music,
found each other and collaborated in my ears.
The sounds that were created kissed my soul.
Remember the first breath of spring as the flowers
opened up their faces and smiled at the sun?
Or a walk in the redwoods after a spring time rain
when the air is crisp and the oxygen so pure?
Your music today accosted my senses and radiated
joy throughout my being. Gone are the days of my
oversensitive sensory system and my soul rejoices.
Notes are allowed to enter me and fill my spirit once
again. Happiness, joy, thrill, dance, smile, relax,
absorb and nourish…these are words of the music
you gave to me today. Thank you for speech that
transcends human barriers and penetrates the life
of this kid. Your talents shared today were a peaceful
bath for my soul.

I have studied the spiritual lives of major composers. Mom and I like to listen to their music and discuss it. I close my eyes and listen, first coming up with adjectives to describe the piece, then I write something about what I hear.

MY LISTENING EXPERIENCE
Brandenburg Concerto
J.S. Bach

Adjectives:
conflict with resolution, moving parts, reinforcing, needing attention, acrobatic

I see a candle flickering in the breeze,
Flickering wildly within the seas.
How can it be? Is what you ask.
Nothing is too great a task.
For God is great
   and God is good.
His praise be endless
   as your reverence should.
Repeat it once again and continue on,
Other keys, other choices, life goes on.
People listen, hear the sound,
His love through Christ to you abound.

MY LISTENING EXPERIENCE
Trumpet Concerto
Haydn

Adjectives:
happy, tuneful, conversational, reinforced

Blowing sounds fly through the air,
A mostly happy tune, I hear.
They talk back and forth,
Those in number and the one alone.
Keep it coming, says the one,
Our dialogue has just begun.
I have so much to say
    that the world must hear someday.
Your voices so strong,
That together they'll hear my song.
You cannot see what making music together
    means to me.

A mighty word to the world;
We must allow each other to be
All unique, with gifts from Thee.

MY LISTENING EXPERIENCE
Die Forelle
Franz Schubert

Adjectives:
wanting freedom, tricky notes, lopsided music

The voice teases me with movements up and down,
Yo-yo like in distance, yet jolly like a clown.
My interest is peaked, the sounds are so sweet,
I give my attention to notes, and I'll keep
    my mind and my heart on high alert.
So, I'll hear you and feel you, the learnings convert
    from mere notes and sounds,
They become love from you,
To share with each other and myself, too.

We all can change the world. You have lips to smile,
arms to hug, eyes to see or a voice to speak. The
most important, though, has not been told;
It's not the cash but the heart of gold.

MY LISTENING EXPERIENCE
Piano Sonata in Bb Major, K333
Wolfgang Amadeus Mozart

Adjectives:
goodness, happiness, time passing quickly, prickly

Stay youthful, the old man cried,
My life today is filled with pride.
Open your eyes and you will find
    much more to life when you are kind.
A look, a hug, a smile, a word,
These are those longing to be heard.
Look real hard at the one in the mirror.
The one you see has Him so near.
To those who have a mirror not,
You're the ones God inside has taught,

Mirror or nor, it makes no difference.

MY LISTENING EXPERIENCE
Symphony #3 "Eroica," Mvmt. I
Ludwig van Beethoven

Adjectives:
longing to be heard, trying hard to resolve things, love despite conflict

An utter grievance shows itself requesting to be heard,
Maybe not as kindly as the song of a bird.
But worth a listen, nonetheless,
And shared by most in humanness.
Can we flourish by ourselves while alone we remain?
My heart says "no" and asks us all to change.
While we can survive, it doesn't necessarily mean
  we'll thrive.
Let's gather up each stray note and compose a
  symphony of hope.
Some will lead and others will follow.
Some need repeating while others are singular
  and take us to a new place within ourselves.
All the while making music played by a society
  struggling to find its peace.
Reigning hope prevails in my heart for us.
Let perfect love enter with each breath,
And the One who loves us will do the rest.

MY LISTENING EXPERIENCE
Concord Piano Sonata
Charles Ives

Adjectives:
intensity, challenging, talking voices

Treat them with respect and they sing together.
Discordance prevails when respect is a forgotten jewel.
Listen to the quiet times, as there can be gentle
    disagreement without discordance.
The crowds shout their angry surprises, begging
    to be heard among the mass of similarity.
Rescue the few who bring light into a world casting
    shadows.
Talk to one another, unless the music is too loud.
In that case, we have no choice but to sing.
The world needs all of its musical notes to compose its
    masterpieces.
Remember, that rests are just as important.

MY LISTENING EXPERIENCE
Piano Music-*Songs Without Words*
Felix Mendelssohn

Adjectives:
discreet, wanting, honesty

Inspired by love for everyone.

Here you take me with you on a nightly flight
   through melodious yesterdays.
Not forgotten but stored for times
   I need a smile or a tear.
They recall the special moments made from love
   between us.
Follow the line of notes through the ups and downs,
To recall the emotions tied together to form our song.
I sublimely await the next harmony,
As it deepens the meaning of our melody.
Christ conducts our recital
   which is open for all to attend.
Please have a seat and listen.

MY LISTENING EXPERIENCE
New World Symphony, Mvmts. I and II
Anton Dvorak

Movement I

Adjectives:
wildly moving, challenging, the leader

"Get in," said the driver. "Be with me for your ride. Can I take you to your destination? Remember the starting point because you leave it forever now. Maybe you will choose to forget about it but it will remain learned and part of who you are today. Over and over I say it. When will you notice?"

Movement II

Adjectives:
sweet in strength, inviting, love

Please, nearer to me come. I am whispering now since yelling doesn't work. I am gentle with compassion but also with an innate power, ruling over all. Can the love conquer the ego in this world? See it – because it can. Strength and tenderness make beautiful music together. Others join you one by one, and our song crescendos. We reach our peak together and the world weeps with joy from its beauty.

MY LISTENING EXPERIENCE
Music for the Royal Fireworks
George Frederick Handel

Adjectives:
majestic, grand, declarative, having respect

There he stood in all his glory,
The one who loved so pure.
His purple light in all it's splendor,
And my soul redeemed, for sure.
Reverently, I listen
As each note makes it's point.
The sounds fill my body,
As no other sound could.
Hallowed be Thy name,
Let this world know,
Your love reigns still.
I love you so.

Part II (gets more lively)
Adjectives:
rugged, happily excited, persistently rowdy,
fantasy at it's finest

I see them running free amongst the redwoods,
The air so crisp and filled with the playful,
   happy endurance of the human race.
They call for us to run with them in harmony and peace.
They are the souls of those we love,
Who speak to us from heaven through mother nature's
   beauty.
Let us all join together in the celebration of life.
For it is truly a gift from God, as is the life everlasting.

Matteo Musso

MY LISTENING EXPERIENCE
Hungarian Rhapsody #2
Franz Liszt

Adjectives:
spirited, dancy, youthful, taxing

That's lust combined with power.
Say to the wind, "Your strength is obvious,
   but how will the banners blow in opposition?"
They defy you as they happily dance instead of cower.
They could rip or fly off in your strength, but instead,
   they accept your swaying as a gift of aerobic exercise.
Rambunctious, then gentle.
What lies ahead as you turn the page?
With the unknown comes curiosity and anticipation.
We tire in your grand expressions, yet are fulfilled
   as our music ends.
We practiced some parts over and over until their melody
   became an expression of ourselves.
Very astute you are, my breezy friend.
Thanks to you, my life will never end.

MY LISTENING EXPERIENCE
Ride of the Valkyies
Richard Wagner

Adjectives:
tremendous power, very aggressive,
luring to defiance

We didn't want to, it just took us,
The wayward voices called us.
The tornado was fierce with words of greed,
Come bask with me, he beckoned.
Together, swirling power is ours.
Announce your decision.
Hurry so your inspiration holds tight.
In the fiery chariot we ascend toward our throne.
Living in a tumultuous whirlwind is painful and
　joy lies in a distant land.
The powerful ride ended all too soon and I yearn
　for love and inner peace – true power.
Trapped am I, vitality is nigh.
Solemnly I ask to turn back the hands of time,
Regretting my greed and my need for speed.
A gentle breath fills my lungs and I awaken in my bed.
Having heard the message – God instead.
The power I seek is planned for the meek,
Distribute it freely, come rescue the weak.
You are loving power.
You are the tornado of kindness.

I went to hear Marc Cohn's concert in Berkeley. This is a letter I wrote to him and the other musicians in his band after the concert. I delivered it to Marc the next night, as we returned to hear the concert once again.

MUSICAL REVIEW: MARC COHN LIVE
Freight and Salvage, Berkeley California

Sunday, April 8, 2018
Dear Marc,

May I call you Marc even though I'm just 14 years old? I was at your concert here (in Berkeley) last night and after the experience I had listening to you and the guys, I feel like we're friends.

You see, I am autistic, so I experience life in some unique, yet amazing ways. I don't speak much with words, but two years ago, Mom discovered a method for me to communicate where I point to letters on a letter board to express myself. Now that I can tell them things and we've gotten to know each other, really, after 12 years of me living in silence, I get to enjoy some of life's greatest treasures.

Mom thought I couldn't handle hearing music because I cover my ears, so we hadn't played much of it for the past 7 years or so. But, that wasn't why I covered my ears, a common misunderstanding of autistics. Anyway, music is one of those treasures to me and your sharing of it last night made my heart sing.

The musical conversations the three of you had on stage proved to all in attendance, that the soul can express itself in miraculous ways and share messages in a way that words alone simply cannot.

As a non-verbal autistic, especially this April, Autism Awareness Month, I want to thank you for how you teach this to the world. Words alone can trick us and even get us into trouble! But with music, words touch the soul, bypassing the ego of mankind.

The emotional ride my soul was on last night was filled with happiness, deep breaths of peace, joy and curiosity as the stories unfolded, both musically and poetically. Even at times when I couldn't understand the words in the microphone, the message was still loud and clear. I think that words are just the accompaniment to the soulful message of the heart.

Thank you all for the "special delivery" of your messages. You've got the US Postal Service beat hands down!

Love, Matteo Musso

p.s. I asked Mom if we could come back again tonight and she jumped on it! So, we'll be out there in the audience, hopefully in the 2nd row. We're going early. I'll be the one with the headphones. No offense, I just need to muffle the timbre of sounds sometimes. I still hear everything.

LITTLE BLACK DOT

Little black dots sitting on a page,
Alone sometimes, yet surrounded by colleagues at others.
Your look never changes even as you age,
Solo, unison, or with others you are arranged.

Little black dot, who made you?
What is your purpose and what will you tell us?
I think you are a language all of mankind once knew,
And you are here for our spirits and hearts to renew.

You may appear innocent as you sit on the page,
But many know better than that.
Those who don't see you but share you onstage,
Use you to connect and with others engage.

Little black dot thank you for coming,
And vibrating inside of me.
With you in my heart, I continue to sing,
Universal language of peace that you bring.

You vibrate a lot little black dot,
Your messages ring loud and clear.
But those rests, oh so quietly alone, do not.
Yet, they make it so dots others hear.

Sometimes it's the silence,
That allows the dot-filled messages to be heard.

SPIRITUALITY, GOD and THE UNIVERSE

Acrylic by Matteo Musso, *"Heart"*

ANSWERING GOD'S CALL

The big red heart is about God's love for us, at the center of His artwork, just as he likes it.
His love expands in all directions, to every size, shape and color of humanity.

Without us doing our part, part of the canvas would remain blank and the beauty would be incomplete.

He wants each of us to make a splash of beauty during our lives and contribute to his masterpiece. We all make the canvas sing, together.   You are a masterpiece.

YOU ARE ALIVE
This was a letter I wrote to a friend who was struggling in this life and ready to give up.

You are alive because we made an agreement, you and I, to deepen your capacity to love.
Some love is taken and some is given during this life.
Know always that you are loved by me and by others
I have sent to you.

Now believe in further opportunities to share love that is in your heart. You have in the past and you've seen its power to transform lives. Are you graciously willing to continue that quest or are you choosing to rest?

You have learned a great deal in this lifetime but there is much more awaiting you. Your friends and family have so much love for you and I want you to feel it in your heart. If you are truly seeking rest, we can make a new agreement.

But while you consider your human options, I ask that you listen to all that your heart has to say. Rejuvenate my child, and we'll talk later. You are loved and I am here.

Love, Your true friend in Heaven.

Acrylic by Matteo Musso
(*Inspired by "Gold Heart Angel," Anita Felix*)

WE ARE ALWAYS WITH YOU

Angels show their strength to us daily,
But theirs is so different from ours.

Man's ego beckons loud arrogance,
While God's angels procure their power from
   His love alone.

Beautiful streams of softness caress us from
   that place of total peace.
In this life, God asks us to let it into our hearts and
   emulate it.

With this idea, we transform from being solely his child,
To being his working angels in human vessels.
And the world is enveloped in love and peace.

Feel love's precious blending of all the colors of your life.

A POEM FOR THE AGES
February 2016, Age 13

A long time ago when the universe was but an infant,
I believed in mankind…an ability to experience
   love in a new way.
I pondered a while or no time at all, in an attempt
   to create you.
A prototype was not needed as I am the Creator
   of beauty and perfection.
A man and a woman, designed by me,
   were given Earthly forms.
Magnificent bodies to house the beautiful souls
   of love energy.
Feel your hands, your feet, and your heart as it beats.
Your brain will be in charge, at least, at the beginning.
The heart will keep the balance between brain ego
   and love energy.
Hitherto, I will always be with you, so fear not.
You are always my child and I, your Father.
The time will come for you to use your free will,
That which I have given to you alone, among all
   my creatures.
You will choose to learn your lessons of love
Or you may get distracted and choose to ignore
   my teachings.

I will help you in your struggles; comfort you in
   your mourning,
Celebrate with you in your victories; encourage you
   in your perseverance.
Laugh with you in your joy; lift you up and
   relieve you of your burdens,
Provide you with prosperity and supply you
   with loving hearts for friends.
All of this is available for you as my children.
Just be sure to come home to me each day.
I will be waiting for you with open arms.
I love you.
Dad

DARK DAYS

Call on him after you laugh.
Call on him after you crash.
Your heart may fail you,
Thank him anyway.
Your dark days will feel heavy,
But have you forgotten the strength of our Lord?
Call on him today,
He'll forgive you anyway.
Cast your demons at his feet,
Your dark days will soon see defeat.

I WAIT
September 28, 2016

My child, how are you doing?
I have been calling you.
Do you have a minute to talk?
I know you are busy but time can stand
    still for our conversation.
I hear your questions and they are so clear.
Why don't you hear my answers?
Goodwill can exist between you and me.
I am still your rock, come and hold on to me.
My victory awaits, it's yours for the taking.
No time is for me but for others you're making.
Remember, my child, I speak in a whisper.
Stop filling your time with all things that are yelling.
You need the softness much more than the loud.
For without the quiet, the loud becomes noise.
In your solitude, seek me, my friend.
And I am here…waiting.

Pastel by Matteo Musso
"Point Reyes LIghthouse"

HIM
2017

Like a lighthouse he guides,
He protects me with his loving guise.
Tranquility around my heart,
He's only begun starting his good work in me,
On display for all to see.
His oceans roar a reverence for Him
Leaving me wanting more,
To understand his greatness,
Just stand before the shore.
Take in what he has to say,
The sight alone is enough to take your breath away.
I have faith to jump in those unknown waters and swim.
I have faith, I have hope, all because of Him.

*I wrote this poem the day after my silent
Shafaw healing session with Master Donadoost.*

THE TRUTH ABOUT SILENCE

The truth talks, the message sings,
You hear it only in solitude.
A message comes, you feel it now,
Amidst life's challenges, it thrills the soul.
Hark, says the author of the silent message,
I'm glad the time with you alone has come.
Good peace I give you while you are listening.
Breathe deeply and let me flood your body with love.
How busy you are with thoughts yet untrue,
That my messages of comfort cannot break through.
Christ has a voice louder than all,
Want to hear it? Just give Him a call.
The minutes and airtime are free to you.
The love and healing energy is, too.
What's in store for you, my friend,
Is comfort and peace that does not end.
Be still my soul, He is the Lord.
To Him I dedicate this every word.

THANK YOU LETTER
TO THE MONKS AT HOLY CROSS MONASTERY
Sunol, California

Dear Father Steven, Father Peter and Subdeacon Lubomir,

Thank you so much for the wonderful and unique experience you gave to me and my classmates by letting us visit your monastery. I found it to be not only informative, but refreshing.

To know that there is such a beautiful and peaceful place where the sole purpose is to worship God and love Jesus, is a blessing for us all.

You see, I am autistic and don't use spoken language much. As I write this to you, I am pointing to one letter at a time on a letter board and Mom is taking dictation. I have heightened senses and abilities that most neurotypicals do not understand. One of them is to feel the energy in my surroundings and actually see colors of that energy.

In a world that's often wrought with bad news in the media, I seek nature and the beauty in humanity to overcome the energetic and emotional upheaval of daily life, which affects me so deeply. Jesus is my best friend. Without Jesus, and God's love surrounding me, I would be insane today.

While I was visiting you, walking on your grounds, experiencing your chapel and learning about your life, I felt the blanket of God's love envelop us. The love energy created at your monastery is like the pebble dropped into the glassy lake.

The ripples of God's peace radiate from you, out into the community and gather abundance to reach the entire world; three men who have chosen to be God's pebbles of love and peace in a world crying out for more of both.

Please know that this guy felt it…and I thank you. Here's a poem for you from me…

PEBBLES

There they live, there they pray,
There they listen to your calling each day.
There they want to be molded like clay
    by you; it's where they've chosen to stay.
Why did they choose a life like this?
No ego, riches or fanciness?
Why do they pray so often each day?
And drop all else to hear what you say?
I know you've called those special ones
    to live lives of great esteem.
For a pebble who causes ripples of love,
It's he who makes you gleam.

Let all who visit this beautiful place be open to examples set there. With God's love leading our lives, may more and more pebbles be cast into that glassy water changing the world back into love, one ripple at a time, according to our individual callings.

Happily yours,
Matteo Musso

I HAVE NO LACK
March 2016

I see the storm,
It is ugly and black.
I see the clouds,
They're ugly on the back.
I see the stars,
Smiling back.
I am God's child,
I have no lack.
I see my mom,
She is not smack.
I see the rain,
I am not stopping at that…
I see God heal me,
He has my back.
I have no lack.

HUMAN CLASSROOM
October 27, 2018

Can't come and go as I please,
The force is just too strong.
Can't free myself in this current state,
The power has waited too long.
Arriving here was an agreement made,
To that I must confess.
But God, be more than just a word
   that flows in times of stress.
He made me to be different,
That makes my life so rare.
So many others live life here
   and want to just compare.
We each are different in our way,
God said that it was best.
So that our lives could be used for
   a learning, not a test.
We're here at school, our classroom's huge,
Who wants to sit up close?
The teacher will surely call on you
   to help more oft than most.
Come sit with me, it's not so bad,
Be brave and know you can –
Affect those in your life He sends
   to you, who need a hand.

The front row grew so immense that war ceased,
arrogance dissolved into humbleness and all the people
ate and drank to fulfillment.

And the world became whole once again.

UNIVERSE CREATED
September 9, 2016

A whirling mass of worldly particles is
 twirling round and round.
Universes collide at colossal speed,
We go along for the ride.

Hang on real tight the driver shouts,
There's going to be a crash!
Keep hands and feet in at all times
 'cuz a BANG will cause a flash!

Kind of serious, don't you think?
To move things, oh so fast?
You might end up with more
 types of life than ever, in the past.

Haha, you're right! God said to them,
"I am the great Creator.
More types of life I want right now
 so I'll say good-bye till later."

And later came in an instant
 or in a million years,
God said, "We're here – live happily!
You'll have both smiles and tears."

Lots of time was made and spent
  but they have not realized
That the time they have is not short or
  long but determined by their lives.

Happy times just cruise on by and
  tough times tend to linger.
Why do they choose that?
  wonders he, it's quite an odd hum-dinger.

You can stretch the happy and shorten the yuck,
It's just as easy to see,
Through eyes of love God's love abounds
And happier you will be.

So now you know, secrets have been shared
with info, what will you choose?

AUTISM

MY FIRST ESSAY
It happened to be Mom's birthday – this was her present.
May 8, 2015, Age 11

The topic of self-acceptance is a hard one. Who knows their true self? I think autistics do. I am not getting stronger by making myself happy communicating more with words, but I am with spelling. I am just me.
I do my best to change. I try to talk, but out comes nonsense. Some day this will change.

I got no more problems than you do, but mine are worse. That is why I see Jesus sometimes. He loves us. I know that. So, the thing to know is love God and your neighbor. That way, you have to be one with God. That way you're yourself.

The end.

THE DEFINITION OF ME
May 30, 2018

I am:
A heart full of love and compassion.
A mind full of ideas and original thoughts.
A soul seeking clarity during this human existence.
A spirit sharing positive energy with those who will accept it.
A teacher to those seeking deeper meaning of life's daily experiences.
A guide for those seeking comfort during life's trials.
A teen wanting to inspire acceptance for all.
A voice for the silent ones.
A messenger sharing loving ideas from our Creator.

I am not defined by any disability with which I may be labeled.
I am handicapped only by those who place limitations on me.
What defines me comes from within my own heart and is
accompanied by the self-esteem which develops as I grow
and am exposed to love and nurturing education.

I define me and others will know me by my actions
and written word.

THE PUBERTY SONNET
10 syllables per line
July 16, 2018

Why, oh why, did you come here, Puberty?
I love being a kid, laughing and playing.
When you arrived, we did not agree much.
Mom and Dad were perplexed by the actions.
Have you invaded my body for long?
Have you decided my emotions flood,
Causing ups and downs for everyone here?
Well, I say to you that I'll play your game.
But, beware that I may trick you, hormones.
I may change from fighting you to freeing,
Letting you surprise me, to expecting.
Then I will release that energy load
And be my loving self once more, you see.
I'm still me, trapped within this puberty!
"Darn it! Let me out!!" cried the teenaged boy.

BRAINIAC WAITS
October 24, 2016

Do you get mad when nobody is listening?
Do you have faith that the body is glistening?
Do you have a way to show your smarts?
Must you wait for their learning to start?

I AM NOT SILENT

I am not silent, be heard my soul.
With faith project your loving goal.
Say what you will through my silent voice.
Your lessons learned by them through choice.
You are my friend, my love, my hope.
Through you we can with all things cope.

Yours in Silence,
Matteo

BELIEVE IN ME
October 23, 2015

I can't handle the constant battle of my body over mind. I am not mad but I can't stop remembering the pain of not being believed in.

BEGINNINGS OF RPM WRITINGS
(Rapid Prompting Method)
August 31, 2016

This was written with the letter board instructor after Mom had left for work, I wrote this to Sara.

I was upset mom felt bad about leaving. I am trying to be less selfish. Mom needs to work to try and support the bigger picture baring RPM takes off. The ability to live comfortably is something I have been taking for granted. Can't thank Mom and Dad enough for the life I've been given.

Can we write a letter to both Mom and Dad?

Dear Mom,

Did I tell you I love you, lately? I mean, I show you time and time again living through hugs. God gives me the inability to use my voice, but the ability to let my actions speak louder. I love you, Mom. I am very grateful and undoubtably blessed for your job. I am very selfish to instigate that you leave your job. God is showing me slowly you try so hard to make me have dang good living. I am learning. Me and the power of RPM are fueled both by helping each other learn day after day about compassion, compromise and a lot of fun is to be had.

Sincerely,
Teo

Halfway through this letter to Mom, Teo wrote this to Sara, this RPM facilitator.

Sara, talking on the board is showing more of independence that I didn't know was in me.

Dad,
Just so we are clear, what you do for me and our family doesn't have a lot of recognition. You are one of my favorite people in the world.

You are the bread and sunbutter to the family.
I appreciate your great job. You give me the help I need to pursue my dreams and your time you spend at work, I am thanking you and thinking of you with so much trust and love. You are a man I aspire to be like.

Sincerely,
Teo

BEING AUTISTIC

I am autistic but what does that mean?
It means I'm full of so much that's unseen.
It means that I'm different than most of the crowd.
Should I be embarrassed or stand up real proud?
I guess that I'd like to be just the latter,
And I work hard on it, but what does it matter?
"We are who we are," is my mantra inside.
"Don't worry so much about blending and pride."

I thank God each day for that little voice,
That reminds me each day, that I have a choice.
"You're perfect, my boy," says a much louder one.
"I'm proud of you and of what I have done."
"I've created some humans who are loving and kind,
Who are brilliant and unique, who'll give sight to the blind."

Autistics are teachers that society craves,
To open their eyes to more simple ways.
We have no choice but to figure it out,
How to find peace and what life is about.

Hurt tummies, loud sounds that escape from our mouths,
Incessant screaming and jumps up and down.
Trapped thoughts held hostage, intelligence waiting,
For someone to see through the façade that's prevailing.

Purposeful bodily actions we share,
All messages for you to receive, if you dare.
You may not want it; many do not.
But we'll keep on sharing, just give it a thought.
It may require some action from you,
A deep inner change or acceptance that's new.

We're persistent and strong, relentless some say,
Also sensitive and knowing but that's hidden away.
We want to have friends but require some things,
Like patience and excitement of gifts that we bring.
Society wants us, they just may forget,
They want some reminders of things that have slipped.
Speaking without requiring a word,
Tweet with your actions and heart like a bird.
Let's open our hearts and release some more love.
For everyone waiting, we give gentle shoves.
We might not present in the usual way.
But what do you want? We're not made that way.

Happy Autism Awareness Month! Let's open up
to all the possibilities life presents. Don't be afraid.
You're safe. We don't have to all be the same.
Autistics forge new possibilities each day.

We'll help you, you just have to let us.

NOTE TO SARA
Sara is one of my RPM communication partners.

Sara, thank you for putting me outisde of my comfort zone. I can get frustrated, but I need a push and a shove and I'm glad you don't give up without a fight. I need to be challenged, not only in what I'm learning academically, but with RPM and with my confidence and courage. I am so starting to trust myself.

I WATCHED HIM

Being autistic is not what it seems.
It's just like being wrapped up in your dreams.
Not all you control, sometimes feels like a movie,
With someone playing you in each scene.

I watched him, that teen making "Martian"
    sounds with his voice.
I observed his ways and compared them to those of others.
He skipped down the produce aisle on the way to get kale –
    they stared.
Sounds escaped his mouth as he enjoyed modern art at a museum –
    they judged.
He didn't say "hi" or look at them –
    they were hurt.
He didn't embrace them long enough –
    they wondered if he loved them.
I watched him, that teen, and saw strength, self-expression,
    bravery and unimaginable patience.
But most of all, I saw love expressed in unique ways.
Did they feel it?

A TOUGH ROAD
I wrote this after I had an OCD meltdown (Obsessive–Compulsive Disorder).
August 8, 2018

Don't turn left, turn right instead,
Neither of us knows what lies ahead.
Neither have been traveled on,
I hope it doesn't last for long.
The monster chases me all the time,
I usually am faster, but not this time.
I hesitated for an instant,
He took me captive in his prison.
I could not shake him, though I tried,
My brain got stuck, my heart just cried.
I lost control and hovered about,
Watching helpless from the cloud.
Mom was a trooper, to say the least,
And she did nothing to unleash the beast.
The schedule changed, the beast grabbed hold,
Of changes that remained untold.
I lost myself amidst the current
    that flowed downstream so fast.
Languishing in such turmoil and
    feeling like I'm going to crash.
Out of control, no grounding there,
Was scary to say the least.
I saw myself turn instantly

Then Mom was done, she'd had enough
    and ran out of ideas,
She just laid down and hugged the pillow,
And then out came the tears.
Ironically, it happened then,
I found my way back home.
My body ached, the adrenaline gone,
And peace was mine to own.
Mom's tears were healing gifts from God,
Streaming down her face like rain.
And I knew then that we'd be fine,
And peace would rule again.
But does it have to be so strong,
This effect of surging hormones?
I pray the answer from God is "no,
The worst has passed, you're victorious."
I pray that Mom and Dad remain
    firmly on my side,
And that they choose to know for sure
    their loving boy's still inside.

To my body: Please adhere to my pleas and respect my family who love us so. I love them more than the words can express.

HOT TIMES IN OUR WORLD

Times are here, opinions fly
    go out the door, look to the sky.
We all are living in this place
    why is it hard to respect one's space?
You think one way and I another,
Needless to say, you're still my brother.
That's why we're put here, so close by,
    to learn we're different, you and I.
So many are fighting and more just feud,
Disgust and judgment they eat as food.
And then we wonder why we're sad,
Then reflect on times when we were glad.
There's always been and always will be
    things on which we'll disagree.
The question becomes, "how will we live?"
And from our side, what will we give?
Let's drop our need to win, win, win
    and let our compromise begin.
The need to dominate who you are with
    disturbs the balance that is our gift.
Within each heart there lies a passion,
A fire that burns us into action.
But don't forget to pack the ice
    that keeps us cool amidst our strife.

PATIENCE IS A VIRTUE, DEAR PARENTS
Age 12

Patience. Patience is vital in the world of autism. I'm positive you know this, but I can't stress it enough. Sometimes we want to give up, parents and kids alike, but I am here to tell you that it's worth the fight! God is my lighthouse and I know He is yours, too. He whispers to me, "Patience my child. It will all be worth it soon." That God of ours finds our weaknesses beautiful. Autistic, anxious, self-hating at times, more better for Him to adore. That is a hope I can cling to. It's vital to treat the least of the vocal as Jesus would. Are you ready to be the little engine that could?

OUR EUPHORIC LENS

Happily in me lives euphoria.
How did it get there? Let me see…

Perhaps I happened to open my eyes
   and things I saw held a surprise.
Do you wear glasses or contact lenses,
   a clearer picture you see?
What's cool 'bout living in this world is
   our visions come individually.
Does that mean that within us lies
   a gift to interpret what we see with our eyes?
And if that's true then what we see
   may differ greatly from you to me.
And if that's true within our eyes
   can we control what inside lies?
If euphoria is a state you seek
   how will you get it when things look bleak?
We all have choices we get to make
   it's labeled our free will.
Although we grow in other ways
   euphoria baffles us still.

If we both look up and see a cloud,
   you may see potential rain.
And I may see a piece of art
   yet the cloud remains the same.
To get that luscious feeling we crave
   let's be our own best friend.
Have patience, love, and will to share
   our hearts and smiles 'til the end.
'Cuz when we share a hug and grin
   it leaves from us one size.
When they receive and pass it on
   it's size just multiplies.
How did I end up so euphoric
   after enduring years of silence?
I let in the love and passed it on.

May the others around us be also willing
to give and receive and together a euphoria
quilt we'll weave. Euphoria lies within our
grasp, we just need to look for the handles.

ANTICIPATION OF JOY
2016
This was a music piece I wrote while getting my merit badge at Boy Scout camp in 2016. I wrote it in the Gregorian chant style.

I await with patience for the future with many things new to me. "Accept the challenge," cried courage to self. Said self, "I shall." And it was so.

Camp explodes with opportunity not small. Self cried with joy, "I wish this joy for all."

DEAR GOD

Teo here. Are you available to chat? It seems I am in need of some help accomplishing my mission. Our contract states that I have a lifetime to get the job done but I am feeling a bit overwhelmed with the assignments lately. I know I can do it, but I'd like more help and advice from you. It's not the giving of energy to those who need it. It's more the cultivating and reprogramming of other's beliefs that exhausts me emotionally.

Bet you could help me remember that it's not for me to decide, that it's your mission and timeline. You and I agreed to sign this contract long ago and I will refrain from asking for a new one at this time. If I am to "save autism," I am in need of help influencing the parents. I thought that would be the easy part, but I was wrong.

Hearing what I say is one thing, but listening and opening up their hearts to changing and evolving is quite another.

Please calm my heart and help me listen to your messages and strategy.

Love,
Your faithful and helpful gardener,
Teo

Ps. Please send fertilizer!

THE WORLD AWAKENS TO AUTISM
April 3, 2017

A problem still prevails.
Pursuing only science ideas will never tell the tales.
A lot's been said about us, that simply isn't true.
So I take it on, the challenge seen, I'll try educating you.
What do you see as "normal?" How is it that life should be?
Should I be just like you? And you be just like me?
My mission is not just like yours and yours is not like mine.
So how then logically can you expect our lives to just align?
What if the brains locked in our heads, only worked one way?
We'd have a billion scientists but no music to hear or play.
If our bodies worked like robots, that'd be no good at all.
We'd have a million quarterbacks but no one to catch the ball.
Humanity was crafted carefully, assembled by a pro.
Our different skills and unique gifts are for the world to know.
Autistics are a unique group with more arriving daily.
Do you really think this is unplanned? If so, you might be crazy!
You learn so much about yourselves but only if you dare to stop the judging and conformity is a challenge beyond compare.
Which of you is strong enough to look inside yourselves,
Ask why it is that you insist we be like everyone else?
We're full of love and accomplish things that deep within us lie.

Just 'cuz they do not shout to you or ask for your reply,
That does not mean they don't exist. We silently succeed.
To live our journeys on this earth, just love and faith
    in us we need.
So this year I implore you to look beyond your sight.
We're not specimens to study from a science point
    of view.
We're love and patience, healing and light,
Sent from God to you.

How does one measure love and teaching when it is
    disguised as autism?

THE INSIDE OF ME
April 5, 2017

How deep will you look and what will you see?
Look past the façade to see the real me.
I am more than actions my body must do
   and likewise, your bodies must do their things too.
Are there ever times when you just can't sit still?
Or you just want to yell something, then you could chill?
We feel that stuff too but imagine this,
That it is so magnified, a great sum like this…
One hundred times ten, then add on three zeros.
To understand this, would make you our heroes.
We just can't contain it, the energy's too great,
So out it just comes, not too soon or too late.
We are sorry if our need for survival sometimes
   conflicts with the schedule you had in your minds.
We do our best to work with these things
   but oft you don't see that, frustration it brings.
I must say out loud, as strong as I can
   'cuz I speak for so many in Autismland.
Remember the things that you notice in us
   are inside you too and seeing them is a must.
For that's when the world starts to shift more to love,
And the earth gets showered with gifts from above.

Accept this and kindness rains down on all of humanity,
as we focus on our commonalities while appreciating
the diversity God so entrusted to mankind.

AUTISM AWARENESS MONTH WRITING
April 15, 2019

Beware, it's here, Autism Awareness Month. Making a month to focus on autism is awesome. Can society see us as integral contributors yet? Many more have been able to this year and I am filled with hope for the future. This year I'd like to write a note about a special tribe of people who often get overlooked by society, yet they bare the brunt of autism challenges. This tribe is called *Autism Parents*. This poem is dedicated to all the parents of autists. May you recognize how special you truly are.

OUR TRIBE
Can you see it? Can you feel it?
   Now it's your turn to shine.
Did you let the heavens know that God
   could make you mine?
All at once we took a leap and jumped into
   your arms,
We knew we'd feel the love from you and you'd
   realize our charms.
For many of you we were a shock, your lives turned
   upside down.
And then for others we eased in gently, and you
   just turned around.
The life of our parents cannot be seen, 'cuz no one
   could believe,
The maze of life you get to forge and secrets you'll
   preceive.
The life consists of all emotions, they range from sorrow
   to joy,
Depending how you view the gifts wrapped in your girl
   or boy.
We feel them all with our big hearts and please know
   this is true,

Not only do we live our lives, we live much of yours, too.
Our parents are our biggest gifts, please treat them with compassion.
They run a big marathon each day doing action upon action.
Help us make friends, cook special food and drive around for miles,
Therapy here, a doctor there, they try to keep their smiles.
They earn a whole bunch of degrees, but none are on that paper.
Biologist, teacher, lawyer, doctor and don't forget peace-maker.
Write IEP's, seek out new ways of helping us feel better,
Our grounding force for safety, emotional anchor and schedule planner.
Even taking us to the store can seem like a mountain to climb,
Others cannot understand, we don't make it sublime.
Remain strong all you parents, stares from others will soon go,
As more April's come around and autism understanding grows.
Not everyone's cut out to lead a life like yours or mine,
But God chose you to give to me and we'll end up just fine.
Your hearts are huge, release your stress so you can enjoy your day
And know whatever decisions you make are stones that pave our way.
Our journeys together evolve with each step we take and we're headed in the right direction because of you, our beautiful parents.

Happy Autism Awareness Month!

MY PRESENTATIONS

LINCOLN CENTER, NEW YORK CITY
April 25, 2018
I was asked to be a "speaker" at the big fundraiser that a group called, "Autism and The Arts" holds at the Lincoln Center. They were raising money for their special month long performance, Big Umbrella Festival, which is held annually.

I am honored to be present here tonight as a representative of autistic people and "silent ones" everywhere. It wasn't too long ago that I was considered to have "diminished intelligence" and a lack of understanding of social cues. I had limited activities in my daily life and most were to forward what my parents and loved ones considered, "my learning."

I have prayed long and hard for this miraculous life I now lead. I was trapped in so many ways: no speech or method to communicate that which I knew, thought, felt or experienced. Can you imagine listening to people talk about you and think they understand why you do the things you do, but are sadly mistaken? Often, I wanted to scream (ask Mom…I did, too) and say, "No, no! You're wrong. I am present even if I don't acknowledge you! I am smart, just teach and educate me. I LOVE music…that's not why I'm covering my ears. I love you, even though I may not be able to make my body tolerate your touch! The wishes I had could be listed in a document longer than the Magna Carta or a book thicker than Harry Potter.

I couldn't draw a stick figure because I had a hard time initiating bodily movements. But now that I have a loving and talented teacher to guide me, I am able to release my inner "De Gaugh" and art mentor in my mind, Matisse. You see, we can do anything if given the chance and taught. We just need people around us to be willing to look past the façade our bodies present and see the potential that lies within. I know the Lincoln Center is all about the arts.

This new program, to bring the arts into the lives of autistic people, is a blessing beyond compare and a gift that will forever be etched into not only the memories, but the lives of its benefactors. You see, the arts are the only things that don't have such "rights" and "wrongs." Our lives are all about such things, as autistics. From the ways we communicate to the ways we enjoy life, are constantly judged by society as "right" or "wrong." That's why exposure to and ways to participate and enjoy the arts, is critical to the nourishment of our souls. If you enjoy a nice concert after a long week of work, just multiply the feeling you get enjoying that concert by 12 million – imagine you went after 12 straight years of work! Then you'll get a glimpse into the journey my soul had last year when I heard the San Francisco Symphony perform live for the first time. I wrote about it in my book and even sent a letter of thanks to the conductor and all the musicians. I sent a silent note of thanks to the composers, too.

So, whatever you guys decide to do to forward this special cause, just know that exposing autistics to life's soul-moving experiences cannot be measured and most will not be able to tell the world what it meant to them. But I hope that after tonight, you'll feel it in your hearts and just breathe a deep, luscious, satisfying breath of "knowing." Thank you for caring and coming tonight. And thank you for the gifts you're giving. Hear all the silent "thank you's."

Your Friend, who's a piece of abstract art himself,
Matteo Musso

While being a speaker at the Lincoln Center fundraiser, I also got to attend their special theatrical production entitled, "Up and Away."

UP AND AWAY PERFORMANCE
MY EXPERIENCE
New York City, April 25, 2018

So away I went just like they said,
My soul and senses to be fed.
The colors bright as they could be,
No shades or mixes, just primary.
The greeting began my imaginary trip,
The welcome kind and the entry, quick.

My body said hello to them as I looked around,
   my heart met theirs, so opened wide and mine
   began to pound.
The songs, the smiles, the eyes wide opened
   lured me ever closer.
Where will we go? What will we do?
My brain needed a docent.
I'd been given two of my own
Their energy full of knowing.
I found my seat in a blue balloon,
The mystery was where we were going.
Up and away on a magical flight,
High up in the clouds.
With things to touch and see and hear,
My senses felt so proud.
When senses get used to carry me,
To a far-off place,
To enjoy a bath of gentleness,
I know God's sent His grace.

UP AND AWAY PERFORMANCE
Continued...

Autistics have an odd agreement,
And not always kind.
Those fickle senses, they take their breaks,
While leaving us behind.
Much of my life is spent like this,
Battling forth and back;
With uncooperative processing tools,
That oft feels like attack.
The show, although quite full it was,
Had quite a neat affect.

While other shows take much more work,
For my system, this was rest.
'Cuz when we rest, we let it go.
A wave of calm and solice,
Envelopes us and sets us free
To make some peace within us.
"Up and Away" did that for me,
I don't know how to thank you.
The gifts you give to autistic kids
Make our bodies and souls feel new.

The Lincoln Center took this kid out of the "sensory jungle" of New York City. Although the "jungle" is an exciting energy, the chance to float amongst the clouds for that one hour was the pillow that summoned my peace. I wish you all your own cloud of peace.

Love,
Your Friend Matteo

This is a "Thank you" letter Matteo wrote to this organization in Minnesota following four hours of presentations he gave to over 300 loving people who work in group homes.

April 1, 2018

Dear Hammer Organization,

Mom and I are sitting on the airplane flying home after a week of Minnesota presentations. I wanted to take a break from watching Big Bang episodes to write to you. I do lots of presentations and have felt the energy of many, but I must say that the collective energy I felt from you as a group, due to the work that you do, was something special.

Maybe some of you came only because you had to, but I felt that most of you stayed because you wanted to. I must commend the work you do each day because I know the teaching methods we use are unconventional and many times, neuro-typical people don't feel like being students. But I'm here to say that in your line of work, you get to learn as much as you want about yourselves…why you choose to do things, think things, feel things inside, judge things and act in certain ways. I know people pay big money at counseling sessions to get these revelations, but your clients will help you discover these things for free, day after day. Cool, huh! I give you a big "thank you" from each of them (as their self-appointed advocate). Here's something special for you:

Love, Matteo

THEY CAME TODAY
*Dedicated to the Hammer Organization
and all of their Employees*

They came in today to assure our care,
They knew that they'd find me, waiting there.
What energy will they bring with them today?
What will we do? Just watch TV or play?
I wonder if they have realized yet
   that inside my head, such deep thoughts are kept.
And inside my heart, different things live,
Such colors of thanks for all that they give.
They may not have known those things yesterday,
But today is brand new; they'll know it, I pray.
I may not be able to tell them with words,
What's trapped in this vessel. It sounds absurd.
There's brilliance and yearning, a thirst for knowledge,
There's intelligence trapped that's worthy of college.
There's an artist, a singer, a gymnast, a poet,
And one who loves people, but just can't show it.

A teacher is in here who's earned a degree,
But not in math or biology.
My degree has been earned in a Liberal Art,
Who's textbook is written from deep in the heart.
And they felt our thanks.
Be kind and courageous, give of yourself,
Put books about judging, back on the shelf.
Attend graciously, the classes taught,
By professors of the heart, you didn't know that
   you sought.
Assume the intelligence and competence in me,
And then you'll be shown who you're meant to be.
If you so desire, that is, way down deep.
You'll recognize our gifts, no more secrets we'll keep.
Discard the box that has trained you so well,
Forget right and wrong ways of communicating and tell
Everyone you know, there are more ways to live,
And more ways to love and still more ways to give.

They jumped out of bed, eager to greet the new day and experience all it has to offer. For it is a gift of opportunity for you and for all those who get to enjoy you.

And bright colors of gold, blue and green surrounded them like a colorful cloud of peace.

And they felt our thanks.

SCHOOL PRESENTATION
JACKSON AVE. ELEMENTARY SCHOOL
Livermore, CA
March 3, 2019

Hi Everyone,
It's nice to be back at this school. I haven't been here since second grade. When I was here, I was the only guy in my class who had autism. I was the only one who couldn't speak with words. I was the only one who secretly understood everything the teacher and students were saying. I had a good time here, and for the most part, people were quite nice. But if I could go back in time and be granted a wish, it would be that I could have made more friends. Kids were nice around me but I felt like they were afraid of me. I was, and still am, a different type of guy. I'm a lot of things, but scary isn't one of them. I understand that the unknown can be scary, so I hope that what you learn this week during Abilities Awareness Week can eliminate most of your fears about those of us who live a life that is quite different than yours.

How is my life different than most?

- My brain learns and processes information using different pathways in my head than most of you.
- I understand math concepts (actually all types of concepts) and patterns immediately.
- I have super-sonic hearing and can zoom in on one voice in a crowd if I want. This comes in handy if I'm interested in someone's conversation if they're across the room at a restaurant. Please know that eavesdropping isn't polite, but I'd get so bored most of the time.

You see, when you don't talk with speech, people automatically assume you don't understand what they're saying, either. But I do and did! So do my friends and colleagues on the autism spectrum! So, I couldn't participate in conversations at restaurants, so I had to keep myself occupied somehow. Listening to other people's conversations really taught me a lot! I got caught up on current events in the world and learned how people communicate with each other in society.

SCHOOL PRESENTATION
JACKSON AVE. ELEMENTARY SCHOOL
Continued...

More ways that my life is different than most.

- I can tell what someone is feeling inside. If you pretend to be happy but you're really not, I'll know. I'm all about pure honesty.
- I have challenges you can see and hear, but have many more that you cannot see or hear.
- Loud, sudden sounds really shock me – like I've been struck by lightning or something.
- Adjusting to new environments takes me a minute, like going in or out of a store.
- Remaining calm when I get frustrated. I've had so much practice with this because I was misunderstood by everyone for the first 12 years of my life. Just because I couldn't take a test like you guys to share or prove what I knew, people said that I didn't understand. They said I was so many years behind my peers in this skill or that knowledge. Can you imagine the frustration? Try putting a band aid over your mouth just for an hour while you live your life and you'll get a tiny taste of what it feels like to be me.
- Sounds escape out of my mouth without my permission.
- I pace a lot to release energy and to feel my legs touch the earth.
- My mind sees letters, numbers and music as colors and I experience food like it's poetry.
- I feel the stress of others and it's really hard.

I could go on, but you have to get to class.

I know my friends with special gifts would enjoy having more friends, too. So, here's a few tips so you can make this dream come true for them...

1. K=KNOW
We may appear different to you on the outside because we don't speak clearly, our bodies may due things without our permission, or maybe we don't say "hi" back to you. But just know that inside, we have the same desires as a kid that you do. Friends, education and compassion, just to name a few.

2. N=NOTICE
Notice when someone is by himself or herself on the playground or at lunch. Approach them gently and invite them to hang out with you. You may need to outstretch your hand to encourage them.

3. O=OPEN
Open your mind and know that there is more than one way to exist in this world. Talking is only one way to communicate – there are lots more. There are many ways to help your body feel comfortable including hand-flapping, pacing, rocking back and forth and letting sounds out of your mouth. They're not weird, they're brilliant solutions to really hard challenges you can't imagine.

4. W=WITNESS
To "witness" means, "to see something." Tell others what you saw and learned this week. Tell them that a person's ability to speak (or not) has nothing to do with their intelligence or the ability to understand language. Tell them we're different, but not scary. Speak directly to us but have compassion if we don't respond. We wish we could and we appreciate you including us.

Now that you know, what will you choose to do?

Join this *"I Know"* movement and be a friend to everyone!

MISCELLANEOUS

ATTRACTION AND REACTION

Attraction, of what are you made?
How do you feel?
Do I make you or is your manufacturing up to
 another?
Can I manipulate you, oh Attraction?
Or do you have your own secret reasons for existing
 in me?
You are so powerful that Reaction often bows to you,
 independent of thought or reason.
You have not been elected, oh Attraction,
Yet your reign is strong and captivating, like an
 unfair Czar.
Sometimes you can be a blessing and other times
 a curse.
Your obedient soldier called Reaction,
 too often follows behind you,
Just as the sheep follows the shepherd.
Reaction is often excused of responsibility,
For it is merely following directives as orders given
 from life experiences.
Attraction and Reaction, I have news for you…
Independent of one another you exist,
Both governed by power so great
 which lives in humans as Free Will.
Reaction, you are governed only by Morals, Ethics
 and one's exposure to Love.

SWIMMING WITH FRIENDS
July 3, 2016
Written after Swimming with Friends

Matteo: I had another pool party tonight. My friends Ethan, Mirella and Nickolasha were here playing with me. We had so much fun in my pool and hot tub. Friends felt comfortable fast. I love the openness and acceptance we share. Parents have fun together, too. Can we do this often, Mom?
Mom: Sure! That's why we built the pool!
Matteo: Good, because it's a dream to be able to hang out. No pressure to do anything in particular, but friends are around to play when appropriate.

A poem for my friends:

LIFE VICTORIOUS
The time together had to end sometime,
I've heard it said before.
It only means our fun today opens to another door.
My dear, dear friends I love you all,
I am so proud to say,
My heart is filled because of you.
You made my happy day!

A Night to Shine is a prom for people living extraordinary lives. I wrote this in the morning after I had attended this party with my friend, Sara.

A NIGHT TO SHINE 2018

I had the time of my life on Friday night! Dressing up in a tuxedo and feeling really special, like a star, was extraordinary. I was greeted by so many friends from this church of mine, I was so blessed. To see familiar faces of joy and love amidst a sea of happy, organized chaos, provided me peace. I want to thank all of you who volunteered at this event. The volume of your smiles, claps and love was even louder than the dancing music. For those of you who weren't there, that says a lot!

FOR YOU

A light that shined for so many of us
    shone bright on Friday night.
The gathering of so many hearts
    could solve our energy plight.
As I got dressed up in my tux
    I couldn't comprehend,
A night so filled with pride and joy
    for me and all my friends.
When I arrived the line was long,
All were wanting in.
Then my turn came to walk the carpet,
The party to begin.

Why do they cheer? Why do they clap?
I really didn't know.
Then as I walked it came to me,
Their love they aimed to show.
I took it in though my feet walked fast.
It may not have seemed I enjoyed it, but I did,
Inside my soul just beamed.
So, God has done it once again,
Created many gifts,
For so many special ones
   whose spirits received lifts!
We could not experience that exact
   feeling by ourselves.
It took you who gave so much,
Working as God's elves.

And the dancing guests replay those memories created that night. They will be forever preserved under lock and key in our hearts. They will be there to comfort us during our challenging times and bring us smiles during our silence. May God preserve them for you, as well.

Love, Matteo "Hot Feet" Musso

MORE LOVE THAN HATE, A 9/11 TRIBUTE
Age 11, September 12, 2016

I meet perceptions from videos and stories about the day we were attacked and I surmise that man alone did this. Under the guise of hate, they came to us with their misguided beliefs unveiled through horror. Lost were thousands among us that day, planting seeds of sadness throughout our nation. Young and old, race and beliefs, occupation and status, male and female, these things that often divide us were all united in non-discriminatory acts of violence. The hate did not discriminate. Hate ensures equality among its victims. Love reassured its power that day. It too, does not discriminate. Love has the unique ability to multiply exponentially. Hate must churn slowly in cauldrons by those who choose it.

We saw it happen before our eyes that day, love's growth and expansion. Humanity around our country and the world united in compassion, action, heroism, prayer, awareness and resolve. Find it today in yourself. How will you share it in a nondiscriminatory way? Brainstorm for one minute in silence. Do you have a pattern in your love? Give it today to someone who is lost or outside your comfort circle. That's the exponent in our algebraic equation of life.

Hate did not win on September 11, 2001. More love grew that day than ever before. Let's honor the lives lost from this earth that day with exponents of love and compassion. Their legacy continues to make this world a strong beacon of love. There is no cauldron big enough to destroy love that is in our hearts.

ARTIFICIAL INTELLIGENCE (AI)
I was asked what my opinion was on the development of AI.
January 24, 2018

Well, it's a conundrum. I believe on one hand, that we've been given the intelligence to develop this type of technology. On the other hand, it's an ethical problem with potentially grave outcomes. It boils down to the most basic question for me: What is the goal? To make life easier? To have more free time? To extend a life? To have a "fall-guy" we can blame when a decision goes wrong?

I am afraid that the more we rely on machines that have no soul, only data input by humans that have their own opinions, the further from human intuition and soul-searching for answers, we'll slip. Why must we be able to read the newspaper while behind the wheel of a car as it drives us to work? As it goes relative to it's uses for disabled people to get around, that would eliminate the beauty of the volunteer who wants to drive us. Opportunities for the best of mankind to help, console, think outside the box and dare I say, the ability to even do simple division at the grocery store in our heads to get the best deal on an item, will drastically diminish.

In summation, I say STOP NOW, before it gets out of hand even more. Robots are fun, but people are more so. By the way, I think vacuuming and sweeping are fun and I don't want Mom to get one of those robots that would take that fun from me.

It's really about perspective, isn't it?

A WELCOME TO FREEDOM
Let's open our gate, let's open our hearts,
Let them come in to where new life starts.
When some have so much and others, so few,
Why wouldn't we share it? God wants us to.
This bridge is a symbol, yet it stands tall
   as a visual reminder, to us all.
Once you sail under and enter its gate,
Acceptance, diversity, love over hate.
These things you must bring, if you wish to receive,
Persecution and judgment, behind you must leave.
Work hard and try, do the best that you can,
And others will come, to give you a hand.
This bridge in its splendor, an architectural treat,
Does more than transport you, to the next street.
They come from all over to stare and take pics,
But will they look with their hearts and
   experience its tricks?
Think deeply about, all this bridge means,
Then turn your eyes inward, to follow its dreams.
A structure of red? No, this bridge is much more.
It's a symbol for us, 'bout love that's in store.
So go build a bridge that takes you away,
From your own misperceptions you've come across today.

Acrylic by Matteo Musso
"Golden Gate Bridge"

Just leave them outside, this Golden Gate,
And enjoy life's blessings. Hurry, don't wait!

And the gate brought them to the home of my loving friends, Anne and Effy. A home filled with a potent blend of kindness, acceptance, joy, happiness, commitment, faith and friendship, all mixed up and aging beautifully in a vat of love, even better than a fine wine.

DEEPENING RENEWAL
Maui Vision Magazine, 4th Quarter 2018

The theme this quarter is Deepening Renewal. I wondered what this meant so I thought about it a while before writing. This is not my usual way, as I most often know immediately what I want to share. I've dug deep and am now renewed, so here it goes…

Renewal is a concept that can be applied to almost every part of being human, from attitudes to our cellular makeup. You can return from a vacation with renewed energy and freshness, ready to conquer the world and you can even renew a magazine or Pandora music subscription!

This renewal concept bounces from being associated with our sacred inner selves to the infinite ways we renew our commitment to capitalism (ie: I even do this by returning to the grocery store with Mom to renew my supply of breakfast bars!). But mostly, I renew my attitude, my thoughts, my dedication to projects, learning and spirituality. I do this daily because I think these are the deeper renewal concepts, which supply opportunities for our growth as human beings placed on this Earth to learn more about love.

So what is "Deepening Renewal" then? It's looking at aspects/activities of your day that grab your attention, analyzing your emotional, behavioral and physiological responses to them and deciding if you like them. If they're not serving you well, this is where the renewal comes in. If you didn't like the types of articles in a magazine to which you've subscribed, I don't think you'd renew the subscription, right? It would just be draining your financial resources for no reason; you're not getting anything positive from that magazine.

Similarly, when we overreact to a situation or blow it out of control, we waste emotional resources. If you yell at traffic driving home from work, how can you have true kindness and patience for your spouse/kids when you get home?

So, when we go deeper in our self-evaluations, our entire being reflects our renewal journey and we are a new self, once again.

LEARNING TO CUT THE MOTOR
Maui Vision Magazine, First Quarter 2018

I love sailing! I don't do it much but the last two times we've been on Maui, we took catamaran rides. There's something about it; you start out with the motor running and the captain steers it in the exact direction he wants it to go. Then, once out to sea, he cuts the motor, puts up the sails and poof, instant peace. The loud, constant hum of the motor is gone, the craft glides gently atop the water. It's buoyancy assuring safety for its passengers and the confidence of the experienced captain sends an energetic feeling of total relaxation, while encouraging a celebratory atmosphere.

Sometimes we forget to "cut the motor" as we live life day to day. When the waves get bigger and more turbulent, we tend to tell the captain, "Hey, move over Buddy! Obviously, I could do a better job steering this thing than you. My plate of appetizers just fell overboard and Mom and Dad's umbrella drinks are running down the seat!"

We take the helm and discover that maybe steering this ship isn't for us after all. Maybe the more we turn the wheel and go against nature and our life purpose, belittling others along the way while elevating ourselves to a place of higher value than them, we wind up in a thunderstorm.

If we can remember that we chose to go on the boat ride in the first place and it comes fully equipped with an experienced captain at the helm, we could all have a chill-out time, relax and enjoy the ride. This doesn't mean that we'll never have to "remain seated for your safety and for that of those around you," or that you'll never lose your appetizer to the sea. It just means you needn't worry about it. You can get another plate of food! And if you listen really hard to the captain, he'll point out the amazing whales and dolphins and you'll have the thrill of your life!

MEMORIAL LETTER TO UNCLE ROBERT NIEMANN
May 29, 2017

Robert is my great-uncle who was a fighter pilot in the Korean war. He was shot down and is MIA.

Dear Uncle Robert,
You really are present today as we reflect on the freedom for which you died giving us. The love you make in Heaven with God is reflected through those of us you left behind. I love your strength, which you humbly combined with bravery and compassion, even for those you were told were the enemy.

What's special about you is the way you chose to serve. You chose your mission, destroying inanimate objects rather than humanity, whenever possible.

A great sacrifice was made when you left your family. Your life was in the hands of others and used for a very specific purpose. When you agreed, God was so proud of you because He knew you trusted Him.

That's the ultimate purpose for our human existence. You experienced His love deeper than most get to in this life because you trusted Him so much that you were willing to sacrifice your life the way you had it planned, for the way God had it planned. How you helped so many live, return home and be free, will never be known by the public, but I know.

I am present with you and have been given the OK to share it with our family. They've evolved enough to understand now.

The rugged life you led in Russia – you had such purpose. When you rode in to save others, you had God with you always. He gave you the intelligence, intuition and courage needed to succeed in your missions.

Uncle Robert, we have never forgotten who you were to us as our family, but just now can begin to fathom who you were and are to God.

Thank you for guarding us and loving us always.

Love and Happily Yours as I think of you,
Little Great Nephew, Teo

LAUGHING

"Funning" is a new word.
Want to use it?
It's silly and laughy
   and rolls off the tongue
   oh, so ravishly.

It's an action word
   akin to a word called "running."
Both are good for your heart
   but only one doesn't make you run!

Tonight I'll stick with "funning," thanks.

EXERCISE SONNET
January, 2017

I learned that a sonnet has 10 syllables per line.

Shall I compare thee to a singing kid?
Thy body remembers the feeling strong.
To want you is not enough, oh feeling.
Thou hast required commitment from me.
Thou hast touched my cardiac system now.
Daily shall I attend thee, Exercise,
For you bear gifts of rejuvenation.
Walking daily and lifting heavy things.
Oh, body of mine these gifts art for thee.
Added joy thou bringst, oh my Exercise.
Really effective results shall be mine.
I willst deliver mine body for you.
Exercise, Exercise where for art thou?
Later today thou shallt mine be again.

HOLIDAYS

A HALLOWEEN STORY

Oooh, Ahhhh, Eeeee,
It is Halloween night,
Kids out getting candy,
And often quite a fright.
I went out
    trick or treating with my friends,
I wish this was the night
    that never, ever ends.
Mom wore a witches hat
    that was colored orange and black.
I was Harry Potter, with my
    Hogwarts robe upon my back.
I felt the magic all night long,
From my house down the block,
And back again I made it home
    before it's eight o'clock.
I still could go for hours more
    from house to house to get,
Milky Ways and Kit Kats, too,
And Tootsies, don't forget!

But I shall not be greedy, no,
That is not quite my style.
Something is calling me right now,
Right there, from my pile.
Mom and Dad think it's enough
    to eat only those five.
The thing that they don't understand
    is that chocolate keeps me alive!
So I must resort to sneaky ways
    of sustaining human life.
The refrigerator in the back
    keeps me from all strife.
I'll see you soon sweet chocolate treat,
Dad put you in the fridge.
You did nothing wrong, do not feel sad
    I'll eat you inch by inch.
Good night sweet treats, I love you so,
Sleep well until tomorrow,
    at which time I'll eat you more,
Without guilt or sorrow!

A THANKSGIVING WISH FOR THOSE I LOVE
November 23, 2016

Today is a day set aside to notice that for which we are thankful. An interesting idea, to say the least, to make a day for this. I hope that as we remember Squanto we can learn from him. He was captured by explorers and taken as a hostage to a foreign place, leaving loved ones and all that was familiar to him. He was often treated poorly but also experienced extreme kindness. He was finally returned to his home only to find his entire tribe was wiped out from disease. He was an interpreter between Native Americans and pilgrims. He also taught pilgrims how to farm and spread peace by developing treaties so all could get along.

How can we take Squanto's lead this Thanksgiving? Love those who hurt us and pray for them. Learn valuable lessons from unexpected changes in our lives. Give the blessings of you to benefit the lives of others. Teach by example, words are overrated. Notice the blessings in everything and every situation. They are always there for those who seek them. Love more and let joy endorphins flood your body.

Here's a little poem I wrote for you.

Love, joy, food and thanks, may all be present here,
Playing our games of reckless praise, so loud that all may hear.
Raising up our joyful hearts not only on this day,
But taking time to notice gifts that you have sent our way.
When we sit down to eat this meal please open up our hearts,
To hear each other even more and love as one, not parts.
For single parts are OK for now and live alone, they can,
But many creatures were formed to blend, and one of those is man.
When each ingredient is added, so precisely to the bowl,
Then mixed and stirred up by the chef, a creation will unfold.
Some may require baking and others marinating,
But rest assured, my loved ones dear, final products are worth the waiting.
Single ingredients are curious, I'm sure you may have noticed,
Some taste sour and some taste sweet, bitter, salty, chunky, treat.
Alone they cannot make a meal, nor a single dish,
Together though, they make new things, complete with this kid's wish.
May everyone today feel loved, accepted for who they are,
An ingredient whose gifts contribute specialties by far.
May we each choose to notice, the blessings in our lives,
And make the biggest gourmet cake, allowing each to thrive.

May God bless each and every one of you today and always.

Love,
Your Friend and Unique Ingredient,
Teo

INFLAMMATION ANTICIPATION
Thanksgiving Thoughts 2017, Age 14

Priceless moments come again when love and thanks prevail,
Very sure God's praise is sung, for gifts he did unveil.
Another year has come and gone, we've mixed both
   joy and tears,
As we do and have so done, throughout life's many years.
It is that time again to gather, with family and friends,
To laugh and feast on nummy gifts that God so freely sends.
There's turkey, salad, bread and gravy, stuffing, beans
   and more,
Please don't forget to bring the pie, or I'll send you to
   the store.
Besides the food, do you know why, we always feel so full?
Reasons exist beyond the meal and are so plentiful.
One thing is for sure that day, when we are all together,
Our hearts have an inflammatory response and swell up
   more than ever.
When that magic organ is so full, it's easy to understand,
There are fewer inches available, for our stomachs to expand!
So elastic pants I recommend, this Thanksgiving Day,
So you can welcome without fear, all love that comes
   your way.

You'll still have room to feast and feast, you'll eat lots on the table,
Let's bottle up that inflamed heart and remember it's inflatable!
Reality is we have been blessed, again we have each other,
And those we love who dine with God, still live in us forever.

May this Thanksgiving season be our opportunity to show others our inflated hearts with smiles, hugs, generosity and prayer. We don't have to be boisterous about it, our actions speak louder than words ever could.

With love and thankfulness,

Matteo

THANKGIVING 2018

THE BOY

There once was a boy who was so thankful for his life. He looked around on Thanksgiving Day and noticed so many things. He wondered why this day felt and looked so different than most. The air smelled savory so early in the morning, some family guests slept over last night, the energy was a combination of anticipation and busyness mixed with relaxed love. Many will travel to join others, yet some will have nowhere to go.

This year the boy notices this more than ever, especially seeing it through natural disasters. Maybe that's why the nummy smells are more potent and the comfort is nestling him like a sleeping bag of cotton balls.

The boy's awareness of God's gifts to him are the only lens through which he'll experience his life today. And when more loved ones arrive later today, the boy will feel his heart swell.

The people noticed more of God's blessings and with gracious acceptance, promised to share them with others through smiles and deeds. And with *thanks,*

Some will eat a lot today, but some will not. Some will enjoy their day while others will be ho-hum. Some will cook like crazy then almost be too tired to eat, and others will arrive as guests adorning the cook with praise. Some will stay safely in their homes while others will wonder where to eat and sleep. Some will be grateful for the gifts and company and others will complain that the turkey is overdone. Some will be in a crowd and another will be lonely.

The holidays always mean different things to different people and thus we experience them uniquely. What we all have in common though is the opportunity to give; love, compassion and even a smile…these are all gifts for us to give to each other. They are truly the gifts that keep on giving.

Many are newly homeless from our California fires, and some have been for years. This Thanksgiving and Christmas season, let's take time to act on our gratefulness, not just talk about it. You know now that I feel words are often overrated. Which one will you be?

SMUIN CHRISTMAS BALLET
December 2017

Mom, I've never experienced anything quite like that before. Forget not an ounce of that sensory treat from yesterday, oh self. Why would you choose to live this life void of such gifts? My greatest sensory adventure took place at the Smuin Christmas Ballet in San Francisco yesterday. It was as if a heavenly baker combined the finest ingredients with the most unique recipe and added the elegance of a watercolor painting to ensure the perfect sensory dessert. A cake that was prepared as a way to enlighten us and remind us of how it feels to let go of all stress and worry, if only for a couple of hours on a blissful Sunday afternoon. My ears enjoyed the naked cake of this heavenly baker. Beautiful music of differing styles, genres and emotional journeys flooded my auditory system. Some helped me escape into memories while others provided opportunity to smile.

My eyes got to experience the frosting of this master cake. The choreography provided a masters touch, acting as glue, securing the auditory experience to the visual one. The grace of bodily movements flowed as a gentle brook through the redwoods on a clear, fresh, crisp spring day. One alone or many in synergy, the movement captured my vision and requested my visual attention. Rambunctious, flirtatious, elegant, meditative; these various movements told me the secrets far better than
any words possibly could.

So, once the master baker bakes the cake and frosts it, it would be fine to eat; even quite enjoyable, I'd surmise. So, would you like your piece presented to you on a napkin without a fork, to eat on the go? Or, are you in the mood for a server to bring you a piece on beautiful china with a fork of precious silver?

The cake and frosting are the same in each case, but the experience is quite different. The Smuin team presented me a luscious dessert and I felt like a king dining on the finest of china. The emotion I felt from the dancers warmed my heart. They frolicked during the fun pieces and fell in love during others. Although just actors of sorts, they convinced my emotions and I happily fell for their story.

Reality is, they portrayed the best parts of our human experience through their performance energy. Lesson learned and felt: if we combine all the best parts of ourselves and mix them together with those of others, we can enjoy a beautiful, sweet life experience. The cake alone is good, but the loving energy with which it is shared, turns a napkin into fine china and a cake into the sensory experience of a lifetime. Pat-a-cake, pat-a-cake, bakers man, bake me a cake as fast as you can.

That's my new prayer for our world. Thank you Smuin team. May many support your gifts and enjoy their true elegance.

Merry Christmas!
Your new groupie, Matteo

CHRISTMAS PRESENCE 2016
Age 13

No, I didn't spell it wrong. What if our society has been spelling it wrong? Changes come when we switch letters around in words, presence to presents. It's actually one of the benefits of the silent autistic who doesn't rely on words – we have no margin of error when it comes to hearing God's message. We feel it and know it. Let's have some fun with this lesson this Christmas and give ourselves the biggest gift of all, inner peace.

What is that, anyway? Simply put, it's being present with God and all that is kind, positive and love. Joy, excitement, gratitude, peace, giving, learning, growing, healing, sharing, discovering, accepting, helping and the list goes on. What if there was an online store where everything was free and all you had to do was enter someone's name and choose the gift you wanted to send them from the previous list? Well, there is, sort of. Any of these gifts are presents from God – and presence of God! Just think about it; if you gave a homeless person a loving smile, which swam in a swimming pool of acceptance instead of judgment, you gave God's presence to him or her. If you hugged someone who was in pain, as if all the love in the world enveloped them, you gave them God's presence. What if God's gift to us at Christmas was the present of Jesus Christ? He gave to us His presence!

What if mankind has been spelling it wrong since the very birth of Christ? How does that change everything about the Christmas season for you? We are now more often talking about Christmas as the "season to give." That's wonderful! What will you give to those you love and those you have yet to meet? What will last longer and be used more, an inspiring conversation about looking for positivity in all situations or a new shirt? A memory-making time between grandparent and grandchild creating a wondrous gingerbread house or a new toy that will soon be outgrown? A special time set-aside during a hectic, busy life for visiting a lonely person, or a knick-knack to set upon a shelf, which will eventually require dusting?

You see what I mean? I am aware that this is not new information but perhaps it can inspire us to place higher value on God's presence as presents to give each other. We usually thank our friend for listening with a compassionate ear when we need to talk about something, then we move on with our lives. What if we chose to see that compassionate listening as God's presence, in addition? Give thanks to Him then bask in the inner peace that follows. Now there's MY kind of present!

May you feel God's presence daily in your life. May you also give presence in a new way this Christmas and all yearlong. The presence of God never wears out, needs new batteries or runs the risk of being returned. And best of all, it's free and easily accessible by everyone through that warehouse of presence that is in your heart. No internet required!
Love wrapped up from me to you!

CHRISTMAS SEASON MESSAGE 2017
Age 14

Months have passed since my last Christmas message. We've all accumulated many additional life experiences; some we asked for and some we didn't, and received anyway. Don't you wish sometimes we could say to God, "No thanks. Did you happen to enclose a gift receipt? I don't really like this one, no offense." Or perhaps we'd already had that gift in a different color or size. Then there's those gifts we look at and mumble to ourselves, "What the heck? That wasn't on my wish list! In fact, I don't even see this as a gift; just a necessity, really."

You know what I mean: socks, kitchen equipment, the stereotyped "bad" vacuum cleaner present. Worse yet, some packages arrive housing things that hurt us, emotionally or physically. Again, I say, "What the heck, Dude? Stick to the list please."

Reality is that God only gives us gifts. I guess once you receive the most amazing gift ever, Jesus, the rest can seem trite or less worthy of our thanks or acknowledgement. But does that mean we should eat a meal without giving thanks or get up in the morning without a smile on our face to greet the new day? Does it mean the socks given to you aren't worthy of the title, The Most Exciting Gift of the Year? Yes, I'll go here, what about the illness or pain? Could there even be a gift in such things?

Often, people feel more love from others during challenging times than when its smooth sailing. A friend of mine, newly diagnosed with cancer, just wrote, "I've said and received more 'I love you's' this week than I have in my entire life!" The gift had been unwrapped and received by him. God envelops us in even more love during those times and sends his angels, both seen and unseen, recognized and unrecognized as such, to those who ask. God is steadfast, so the asking isn't even necessary. God is always with us. Our asking just helps us be more a part of the process and brings us more awareness of His presence with us.

So, as you shop for gifts to give your loved ones this year, have fun and enjoy it. The biggest and most relevant gift has already been given to them in Jesus. No offense, but the rest is just "fluff." And who'd ever let 'fluff' stress them out? God won't ever enclose a gift receipt, I'm afraid. But what He assures us is that gifts can always be recognized by us through our innate ability to see, receive, acknowledge and transform.

Remember that love is the greatest gift of all. That's when "re-gifting" is the best thing to do!

Happily Yours and Merry Christmas!
Matteo

ADVENT MESSAGE 2018

It's here again! While I like the decorations, concerts, music everywhere and the gatherings, that which excites me most are the possibilities that the Christmas season brings.

We get to see how people think about others a bit more (bell ringers, Toys for Tots, food drives, etc). Well, I think it's exciting! When people think about, pray for or help others, I see pops of colors bursting from them.

My synesthesia (a neurological trait) allows for this and I love it. If you could see what I see, you'd be praying even harder and more often that we love one another; strangers, family and friends. Walking down the street seeing people smiling, saying, "Happy Holidays," "Merry Christmas," "Happy Hanukkah," etc, is like seeing a beautiful Fourth of July fireworks show, in December, in the middle of the day! It's really pretty. Add in the music, with its vibrations actually tickling my sensations and you can see why I love this season.

God loves the loving, thoughtful energy we release during this season, too, although society has drifted so far from His original intent for Christmas. Can you believe that? I think its His sneaky way of exposing those who may not be close to Christ, to feelings that we all as humans, crave; love, acceptance, joy, giving, and inner peace.

If we don't know God and Christ, we may only experience these feelings on special occasions, or be void of them altogether. They may have been replaced with tangible things or one may have resigned oneself to a lonely or hopeless life.

But Christmas season comes on schedule each year and the joy that resonates from those who know its true meaning, blends with the "special occasion" joy from those still wandering in the dessert. Then God smiles as angels share the news of His ultimate gift, and some of the wandering return home and are lost no more. It happens all the time; we just don't always get to see it.

If you talk about the "real Christmas" at Starbucks with a friend as you're radiating joy that is in your heart, you just don't know who may be eavesdropping, what they learned and how the Holy Spirit worked its miracles.

May "special occasion joy" be transformed into pure, everyday joy and inner peace, both for us and those secret eavesdroppers God places in your path. God, please let me be one of your joy-filled angels this Christmas season, a spark in your fireworks show, and always. And thank you once again for your gift that keeps on giving, Jesus.

Merry Christmas!

NEW WORDS TO JINGLE BELLS

Family tales, family tales, Funny all the way.
Oh what fun it is to tell, stories of each day.
Family tales, Teo tells, boy I have a lot.
G'ma, Papa, Uncles, Aunts, and cousins in the plot.

Flyin' home to see, my friends and family,
Minnesota snow, and Emmie and Madi.
Lake City isn't far, we drive there in the car,
Team Teo meets and thinks some more
    and plot a Holy score, SO…

Family tales, family tales, Funny all the way.
Uncle Mikey singing loud a song that takes all day.
Friendship tales, Teo tells, school is so much fun.
Zumbrota has such special kids, I'm the most blessed one.

A day or two ago, to Anne's sixth grade I went,
I met some more new friends and there two days I spent.
Classes and roller-coasters, Secret Santa, gifts and gym,
A talent show, true gifts displayed but no one's name was
    Kim! But…

Family tales, family tales, they'll come flowing out.
Mom dictate this every word, no editing allowed.
Papa's cane, what a pain, why won't it stay up?
G'ma's walker gets around and she still keeps her cup
(in the fridge).

Presents and gifts we wrapped, we didn't spend too much,
The true gift of self, is more than just a crutch.
We can lift up our friends, inspire with our hearts,
And God will be there all at once and then the healing
    starts!

CHRISTMAS MESSAGE 2018

LOVE IS HERE
Love is here, it grows so bright
   in person, arrived that Christmas night.
A baby boy who God has said
   would be our teacher, by Him be led.

Love as He did, teach as He does
   and treat each other kindly, 'cuz
   when you do this throughout the year,
Your heart will carry God's Christmas cheer.

And the star that shined so bright that eve,
lived in their hearts forever…and all was well.

Merry Christmas and Happy Every Day After!

OH CHRISTMAS TREE
December 10, 2018

Oh Christmas Tree, why do you gleam so majestically? Why do they dress you with lights and ornament your natural beauty? You are the vision that excites little children as they see your glow for the first time each year.

I admire your agreement to sacrifice your life for our nostalgia. Is there more? Perhaps that's why we stand in awe of you and your perfect glow.

As we absorb its warmth, our hearts swell and memories fill our souls. Your lights aren't just bulbs,
But rather, sparks to inspire us to love each other
    and remember that first spark God sent us as His son.

The living example of love incarnate.
The ornaments are memories,
Old and newly created,
That comfort us and bring a smile.
Thank you, Oh Christmas Tree.

I will be a spark and will emulate your beauty
in the world as I live each day of the year.

CHRISTMAS EVE MESSAGE 2018

"Hi! You've reached me. Please leave a message after the beep." Sorry to miss you but I'll leave you a very special message today. Now that I have your attention, here it is; today I am giving you and the rest of humanity my love, encapsulated in a baby. You've seen many babies over the years, and most of you thank me for that precious bundle. But this baby? I don't want a quick "thank you" note. I'd prefer action over words for this one. He's more than a healthy baby with ten fingers and ten toes. He's going to grow up to be your teacher by example, a humble servant, a miraculous healer and all positivity that I wish humans to experience in life. He'll have faithful friends and an extremely meaningful mission. He'll teach about my will and my love for you. The "thank you" from you would come in the form of following Him and emulating his love with each other.

POPCORN IN THE SKY
Dec.17, 2018
I wrote this on the flat letter board with Sara, (meaning that no one was holding the board for Teo), as a New Year's Eve message.

The star's youthful glow lingers with spectacular dance and assurance that says that right here is God's taste of a "twinkle in the eye" for us on Earth. Continue the sparkling balls of fire, I pray; for it reminds me that even stars start all over, but first with an explosion and a new glow, just as I start my own glow for the new year.

We all have our glow, so let's take inspiration from the stars. All we can hope for is our glow to grow.

HAPPY "KNEW" YEAR!
January 1, 2019

That which has passed is gone; all those hours,
They've left us with so much more learning.
The new year is here, we know it's been coming,
Let's greet it with excitement and yearning.
Did we know what would happen in 2018?
Do we know what lies ahead?
Would we like to be privy to each detail,
Or be surprised instead?
Each surprise brings us options, whether asked
 for or not.
Then we take what comes next, adding it to our pot.
Next come reactions, then the learnings follow,
What we know today becomes what we knew,
 tomorrow.
This 2019 let's take what we knew and apply it to
 every day.
We knew smiles, hugs, helping have brightened
 the day,
Of loved ones and strangers God placed in our way.

Starting fresh each year is fun. Let's combine the old and the "knew" to bring peace to the world, one smile at a time.

EASTER MESSAGE 2017

Our world has a keeper. I feel His breath. "Can you give me your life?" he asks us. "I gave you mine to show my love for you and to exemplify true knowing of Heaven. I ask you to give your life to me but not in the same way. Be joyful, worry not, love others, accept one and all, know I live, seek the good always, laugh, uplift, meditate, breathe, care for each other and the earth. In doing these things, you are mine."

The cross has served as a symbol of Christianity for thousands of years. I wonder why it has to separate us from other lovers of God? Christ did not intend to cause dissension, but rather to bring us all to God. That was His mission. Man chose to let his ego and need to be right cause the separation of religions. This Easter what if we Christians chose to wear our crosses as a symbol of loving and knowing God? Not as a symbol setting us apart from Jewish, Muslim, Buddhist people, or any other defined belief system? How would the energy shift? Judgements could vanish and be replaced by unity! Our scrutiny of others could be replaced with acceptance! Our self-righteous indignation could be replaced with humbleness! Wow, imagine THAT world!

Close your eyes and see it. What would be in the news? It would certainly look different than it does today. Let's all visualize it and KNOW that God and Christ can do anything!

The crosses we see can be made out of anything. Some are old and some are new. Some are jeweled and cost a lot of money but some are simply pieces of wood tied together, or even sticks. They come in all shapes, sizes and colors. Notice that they all intersect at a point in the middle and that is the strongest point of the cross.

God is very clever in his messages and has had help from man in developing them in such a variety of ways. These man-made crosses all over the world continue to intersect in the middle.

I've listened and heard the truth. When the cross is worn or seen as a teaching of God's word, we are unified, not divided. If the cross isn't connected somehow in the middle, it becomes just two separate sticks. Christ became the glue or rope that holds the two pieces together.

Hear this please..

ALL FOR ONE AND ONE FOR ALL

Come to me, God said to humanity
And I will love you 'til eternity.
Will you except me on the earth?
I restored your souls through Christ's own birth.

Call me by any name that's love
   and I will listen from above.
Holy God, Universe, Energy or Christ,
They all are me, not one's just right.

I must remind my children now
   To judge and fight is just not how
   To live as we agreed you'd live.
This life's about just how to give.

ALL FOR ONE AND ONE FOR ALL
Continued...

Just give? you ask, that's all I do?
Shouldn't I receive some too?
My child, my dear, what you must learn
   that it's by giving that you earn.

Give of your gifts, your means, your time,
Give of your life, your love, your mind.
That will be a wonderful start
   as you strive to give your heart.

This Easter time let us reflect
   on those things we've hidden, chose to neglect.
Open minds and open hearts,
Christ on the cross is where this starts.

EASTER MESSAGE 2016
Easter fill in the blank, my words are in caps, then the following message.

Easter is a time of CELEBRATION.
My favorite part about Easter is FINDING THE TOMB EMPTY.
Easter to me is BELIEVING CHRIST TEACHING US TO TRUST GOD NO MATTER WHAT.
The world CAN CHOOSE TO HAVE GOD'S LOVE BEYOND UNDERSTANDING TODAY.
To celebrate, we should SING, SMILE, LAUGH, CARRY LOVE TO OTHERS AND HAVE A CAKE POP.
I am happy because WE CAN CELEBRATE CHRIST IN FREEDOM.
I think ALL FRIENDS IN CHRIST ARE VERY BLESSED TO PAY HOMAGE TO GOD.

EASTER MESSAGE
Will you celebrate with me?
Such love has come down from the cross.
I have good news for you.
Will you listen with your heart?
When they killed me, energy ascended.
I made a path to Heaven for you.
"Follow me" means many things,
The paths are heavy trodden.
The ones on Earth and that to Heaven…
I have cut back the brush
And the way is clear.
I shouted from the cross so humanity could hear.
Rejoice today, I've freed you all,
Now please go and heed my call.
I love you all and so I bled
So everlasting life to you be fed.
Yours Eternally, Christ

I HAVE A DREAM 2019
Celebrating Martin Luther King, Jr.

I have a dream…
That the world will be a place of peace and joy for each human and animal.

I have a dream…
That actions will reflect the Golden Rule in each of us.

I have a dream…
That each person will be fed with both food and spirituality.

I have a dream…
That people will recognize how good it feels inside to help another person, then be driven to re-create that feeling again and again.

I have a dream…
That love will become the dominant emotion and that compassion will be our inspiration to bring comfort to all humanity.

I have a dream…
That people won't be segregated into groups, rather, we all realize that God created each individual person with unique gifts to bring to this miraculous party we call "life."

I have a dream…
That each and every person be invited to and welcomed to this party, rather than be told that they don't belong.

I have a dream…
That all of humanity opened its eyes the next morning and saw all the colors of the rainbow and many more between the stripes… that only eyes filled with love and compassion can see. Dreams can come true!

After watching Martin Luther King's "I Have a Dream" speech in its entirety. Every word he said is true and moral. I enjoyed his speech because he spoke for so many who needed a voice. I am sad that such a moral leader was taken from this country so early in his life. We sure could use such a moral leader now. Part of me is like him; I feel a closeness of passion and ethics. Let me see...

I HAVE A DREAM, TOO
January 17, 2018

I have a dream that someday people of all races, religions, sizes, persuasions, languages, talents, intellect and speaking abilities will be respected and accepted for what lies within their hearts, not for how they fit the "status quo."

I have a dream that all people will use the language of actions over speech; that bold, humble service and giving, shouts louder than saying what was done.

I have a dream that the need for words that say, "I love you" disappears into the smiles shared, hugs given and good deeds done for those we love and for those we have yet to meet.

I have a dream that flowing streams continue to provide basic essentials for mankind and the cleaning of the environment proceeds in bright success.

I have a dream that nations can realize that no piece of land is worth the killing of so many and no matter what man's ego thinks it knows, God still requires us to put love first.

I have a dream that people turn from judgment and fear to mutual respect and trust.

I have a dream that education will be given to everyone, whether they can communicate with words or not; that the intelligence and competence of people are not judged by their visual displays of harmless movements or actions.

I have a dream that the beautiful plan God had of blessing each of us with gifts that are to be unwrapped and shared, will be discovered and nurtured for the betterment of society.

I see this dream coming true in my heart. Let it be so. And a warm blanket of peace and prosperity covered the Earth in a bed of love and respect.

MY BRAVE NEW FRIEND
September 24, 2017
In honor of our troops.

Thank you, my friend, you are so brave
Your time, gifts and bravery to us you gave.
You've left the comforts of home behind
For the freedom and safety of all mankind.

Why are you willing to do this for me?
Risk your life and your comfort for even those
    who can't see.
I think I know why, or at least I'll guess...
You think more about others, and about yourself less.

Democracy is important to you
It is also to me,
And to thousands of other people,
Who only dream to be free.

With a big sense of purpose and all the right training,
Off to battle you go.
Just know in your heart, your mind and your soul,
That we're with you, more than you know.

And God sent his angels to protect them and help them feel our love.

Your new friend and professional pray-er,
Teo

VETERANS DAY 2018
Thank you to all. With the sincerest respect and admiration, I say to families and friends of veterans and the heroes themselves, you are truly admired with grateful hearts, and your bravery and efforts should be observed on such a special day. God made you brave and you honor God by using your bravery to protect and defend us. You've never met most of the recipients of your precious gift, so I'm sending this message out to the world with the hope that everyone will take a moment to read it today and as they do, you will feel our collective thanks and gratitude.

YOU ARE BRAVE
You are brave. Your caring for freedom is evident: We voted, prayed and spoke our beliefs because of it. Your longing for security is a priority: We sleep while you protect. Your love of America is beautiful: We often take for granted that for which you risk all. Your sacrifices cannot be fully realized by us, but they are enormous: We cannot imagine.

Your expertise in what you do is professional: We are thankful. Your commitment is admirable: We can enhance ours by learning from yours. Your strength is powerful: We pray for it's wise use. Your trust in each other is pure: We are too often, skeptical. Your faith is unstoppable: We have too many opportunities to let ours waver.

Our American Dream is possible because…
You are brave. Thank you from our hearts. Feel it from us each time you close your eyes at night. God is with you and protects you and your bravery and in so doing, graces us all. With a Grateful Heart,
Matteo

MOM'S ARE BEAUTIFUL
May 5, 2016
Mother's Day Prayer/Poem

Mom's are beautiful, God's gift to kids,
With all they are, life to us they give.
So many times we tire them out,
Their love remains without a doubt.
Some moms are funny and some serene,
Some play real hard and others clean.
Mom's care for us as best they can
    while learning themselves from Christ, as man.
Love comes to us in many forms,
The way it's given through all life's storms
    depends upon our unique needs,
God planted in us as little seeds.
God's love delivered through their care,
Radiant and hopeful strength they share.
I thank you God, Mom's love resounds,
Embodied so your love abounds.

ABOUT THE AUTHOR

Matteo ("Teo") Musso is a 15 year-old young man with autism. They continue their journey together working on his verbal abilities but for now, he continues to communicate through his letter board, expressing himself beautifully, one letter at a time. Matteo lives with his parents, Mark and Annette, in northern California.

Matteo is a "teen on a mission," spreading what he calls, "the truth about autism." He's an inspirational speaker and has shared his messages of love, hope and truth about autism to over 8000 people during the past three years.

When Teo is not writing books, traveling to speaking engagements or working on his YouTube Vlog, *Monday's With Matteo*, he enjoys learning – about everything! Math and Physics are his "fun" subjects but he enjoys studying all of them. Swimming, shooting hoops, hiking, Boy Scouts, camping, working out, drumming, music, art and hanging out with family consume the remaining hours of his daily life.

But don't forget food! He loves to make it, eat it, then write about it as the *Poetic Foodie* in the *Teo's Tasty Adventures* section of his website. Come and visit and be sure to check out his other books: *Handbook of Us: Understanding and Accepting People with Autism, Loveland* and *I Am Yours*.

www.matteomusso.com
YouTube Channel: *Matteo Musso Official*

Made in the USA
Columbia, SC
08 May 2019